LET THERE BE LOVE

LET THERE BE LOVE

Gillian Stokes

MQP

MQ Publications Limited
12 The Ivories, 6–8 Northampton Street, London N1 2HY
Tel: +44 (0) 20 7359 2244 Fax: +44 (0) 20 7359 1616
email: mail@mqpublications.com
www.mqpublications.com

ISBN: 1-84072-976-7

1 3 5 7 9 0 8 6 4 2

Printed and bound in China.

CONTENTS

INTRODUCTION

LOVE IS GOD'S GREATEST GIFT TO MANKIND. Love seeks nothing for itself and makes both the lover and the beloved feel wonderful. Jesus taught by example what it is to love without conditions. Throughout the New Testament we see examples of His selfless compassion and mercy to allcomers, regardless of their social position or state of being: He loves equally the sick and the well, pillars of the community and social rejects.

JESUS PAID PARTICULAR ATTENTION TO anyone with a strong faith or a burning desire to hear him speak, and he showed that such faith and determination will always be rewarded. Jesus is the ultimate example of generous, constant, and unselfish love. A love so simple and so strong that he willingly sacrificed His own life to atone for the sins of mankind. I hope this book inspires you with His example. In it you will find ways to bring a loving heart into your home and workplace, and practical strategies to help you solve more challenging questions, such as how to extend love equally to enemies and friends, and how to find the love in loss. Today is a good day to learn more about God's love.

"Charity [love] suffereth long, and is kind; charity envieth not; charity vaunteth not itself, is not puffed up, Doth not behave itself unseemly, seeketh not her own, is not easily provoked, thinketh no evil; Rejoiceth not in iniquity, but rejoiceth in the truth; Beareth all things, believeth all things, hopeth all things, endureth all things."

1 CORINTHIANS 13: 4–7

PART 1

Loving Relationships

GOD IS WITH US, AND GOD IS LOVE. God is never further away than the blood in our veins or the air we breathe—but perhaps you have been too busy looking for love elsewhere to notice Him. Whether our spirits soar or we feel depressed, God's loving compassion is with us all. We are part of His creation and He reveals Himself and His love through us just as he does through any external object, person, or event. To become aware, we just need to pay attention. Here's how.

"...God is transfiguring the world right this very moment through us because God believes in us and because God loves us. What can separate us from the love of God? Nothing. Absolutely nothing."

DESMOND TUTU WITH DOUGLAS ADAMS

GOD IS LOVE

AS A CHRISTIAN SOCIETY, OUR MODEL OF LOVE IS inspired by what we know of God's love for us as revealed through His son, Jesus Christ. Our awareness of Christ's life and teachings shapes the expectations we have of a loving relationship, whether we believe ourselves to be Christian, agnostic, or atheist. Our very concept of the attributes of love is drawn from Christ's example: He is compassionate, patient, honest, non-judgmental, all embracing, consistent, merciful, charitable, self-sacrificing, perfect...the list could go on. It's these attributes that are shared by love of all types —romantic, maternal, brotherly and so on.

THE EVIDENCE

IF YOU DOUBT THE ASSERTION THAT GOD IS LOVE, stop for a moment and, as an intellectual exercise, contemplate the questions posed opposite. Write down your thoughts on a piece of paper if it helps. After thinking for some time about the answers and the issues they raise, you might come to the conclusion that love is God, and its corollary—God is love. The concepts are indivisible in the human mind, and so to deny God, it seems, is to deny love itself.

Questions to Ponder

- ❖ How you would feel about a God who was occasionally partisan, fickle, inconsistent, or deceitful?

- ❖ Could the actions and attitudes described above be thought of as Godly?

- ❖ Can you find ways to define or describe love other than by the attributes Christ exhibited in his life on earth?

RETURNING TO THE SOURCE

AMONG OUR INNATE ATTRIBUTES, WE ARE BORN with a desire to return to God. We all have a longing to return to a state of union, and believe we can satisfy that desire through intimate human relationships, fusing with and losing ourselves in a beloved other. We long for a love that knows all about us (even the parts we feel ashamed of), yet continues to accept, love, and cherish us. We would not knowingly seek out a shallow, selfish love that took but did not give in return. But as adults, when we strive to satisfy our longing for perfect union through an intimate relationship with another person we are doomed to disappointment, since perfection does not exist this side of heaven.

"We seek in romantic love to be possessed by our love, to soar to the heights, to find ultimate meaning and fullfillment in our beloved. We seek the feeling of wholeness. If we ask where else we have looked for these things, there is a startling and troubling answer: religious experience...."

ROBERT A. JOHNSON

WHAT IS LOVE?

REAL LOVE DOES NOT CRITICIZE OR DEMEAN, even when disappointed. It seeks to give, not to get. It loves the other for who and what he or she is now, not for what they may become, nor for what we think we can make them into. We are all fallible at times—we are human after all—so, inevitably, we fail to live out the projected or imagined persona our partner wants to cloak us in. No matter how loving the bonds we form, human love is limited when compared to the love God bestows so freely everyday. You might think we would be better off if we gave up on human love, given that it is so flawed. On the contrary, Christ taught us that to love one another is the most important of the commands God has given us. If we do nothing else in life, we should love each other no less than we love ourselves. Jesus Christ taught that of all the possible human attributes, love is the greatest.

"God loves each of us as if there were only one of us."

ST. AUGUSTINE

"Though I speak with the tongues of men and of angels, but have not love, I have become sounding brass or a clanging cymbal. And though I have the gift of prophecy, and understand all mysteries and all knowledge, and though I have all faith, so that I could remove mountains, but have not love, I am nothing. And though I bestow all my goods to feed the poor, and though I give my body to be burned, but have not love, it profits me nothing. Love suffers long and is kind; love does not envy; love does not parade itself, is not puffed up; does not behave rudely, does not seek its own, is not provoked, thinks no evil; does not rejoice in iniquity, but rejoices in the truth; bears all things, believes all things, hopes all things, endures all things.

Love never fails. But whether there are prophecies, they will fail; whether there are tongues, they will cease; whether there is knowledge, it will vanish away. For we know in part and we prophesy in part. But when that which is perfect has come, then that which is in part will be done away.

When I was a child, I spoke as a child, I understood as a child, I thought as a child; but when I became a man, I put away childish things. For now we see in a mirror, dimly, but then face to face. Now I know in part, but then I shall know just as I also am known.

And now abide faith, hope, love, these three; but the greatest of these is love."

1 CORINTHIANS 13

SWEET SENSATIONS

THROUGH THE LOVE WE EXPERIENCE IN HUMAN relationships we feel a reflection of divine love. Love is not just an abstract notion; it demands to be realized through action and feelings. The intimate relationships we form with family, friends, and lovers allow us to experience the selfless devotion, surrender, and passion that will bring us closer to God. As the strong feelings of the faithful who clamored to hear Jesus speak, or were sure he could heal them or raise their dead testify, Christ responds to strength of feeling and faith: a feeling state, not an intellectual idea.

When we feel the urge to know unconditional love from other human beings, what we experience is merely a hint of the innate desire we have for God, whose love is absolute. The passion we feel for a lover is drawn from our inborn passion for union with Him. All our lesser loves are but pale shadows of that greater light. Although mankind's love is tainted by limitations and imperfections, and is conditional in nature, we continue to give and receive human love because Christ taught us that it is through loving each other that we can learn to love God. His face is the face of all lovers, and any heartfelt love takes us nearer Him.

FREE LOVE

WHEN LOVE IS PRESENT WE ARE ABSENT. ONLY the beloved exists. All thoughts and feelings are focused on the object of our love, not on ourselves, whether for a fleeting moment or a lifetime. Love is revealed in expressions of understanding, acceptance, and tenderness. At other times love expresses itself in firm action in a moral cause. Knowing the difference between loving action and the distortion of spiritual values to suit personal or political motives requires honest discrimination: If we can picture Christ acting the same way we will not be far from the mark. Love wants for the beloved all that he or she wants for themself, even if this doesn't include us, and even if firm resolve is required to enable the lover to achieve it. Love that tries to smother and possess is not love. The desire to grasp and control is motivated by fear. We fear the loss of accustomed things, lifestyles, or people when we relinquish control, yet true love is never tight or closed. It enables and allows in faith that all is as it should be. We deny God's will when we insist on things being our way or no way. Perhaps God has better things, lives, or people in line for us. We'll never know if we shut out the truth. This is not to advocate accepting another's will if it goes against our own. God gave us freewill. He does not ask for victims or doormats, but for conscious individuals who freely give love and are free to withhold it if they choose. This loving discrimination has been compared to a bridge of hair crossing a chasm of fire. When we step away from loving actions toward selfish ones we know it, if we have any self-awareness.

"Love has no meaning if it isn't shared.
Love has to be put into action.
You have to love without expectation,
to do something for love itself, not for
what you may receive. If you expect
something in return, then it isn't love,
because true love is loving without
conditions and expectations."

MOTHER TERESA

WHERE IS LOVE?

WHEN WE LOOK FOR GOD WE FIND HIM. HE IS present in every smile, in every blossom, in every pain. There is nowhere He is not. We find what we seek. God is love, so it follows that love is also present in all things: in the events, people, and objects we welcome and in those we do not. Since energy follows thought, if we look for failure and disappointment they will surely be found, but if we look for the good in people and situations, and search out signs of God's love, we find that they abound, both without and within us.

"When love isn't in our lives, it's on the way. If you know that a special guest is coming at five o'clock, do you spend the day messing up the house? Of course not. You prepare. And that is what we should do for love."

MARION WILLIAMSON

LONGING FOR PERFECTION

DESIRE FOR HAPPINESS IS A POOR SUBSTITUTE for a stronger force of attraction—our desire for love, which is the desire for God. It is not easy to recognize the stronger force when we are seduced by the many manifestations of its substitutes. We live in a tangible world where we desire and love so many things that the heart becomes like a hotel. We love this artist, that TV program, this film star.... Behind each desire is a longing for perfection, a sense that there is more. As we blindly covet and acquire there remains a belief, deep down, that there exists a greater perfection.

THE ROMANTIC HERO

TO IDEALIZE ANOTHER PERSON IS TO SEEK OUT IN him or her the perfection of character and beauty we suspect we lack ourselves. Believing we have found it in our romantic hero or heroine, we imagine ourselves made complete. But no human relationship can sustain such an illusion for long. If we are lucky, obsessive desire is replaced by lasting companionship, appreciation, and loyalty for the other as he or she is, not as we need them to be. The drive to achieve completion and find perfection in another human being veils a desire for the one perfect love, which is God.

"…If I find myself loving a person it is only because I am trying to find, in and beyond that person, the God who is Love. In the person who loves me I discover the one who loves me most. Because I love, I experience from that other person just a little bit of the way God feels about me. In the person who attracts me is the God who is drawing me. When I find a person I love I always take it as a message of God's love. The more you love, the more messages there are."

CARDINAL BASIL HUME

LOVE REVEALED

WHEN A GENEROUS ACT, A KIND WORD, A SMILE, or a tear touches you, God reveals Himself to you. Learn to see his many faces and notice how he is always sharing His love with you. We are surrounded by love at all times, though too often we overlook it. We turn away, distracted by modern life with its enticements and worries. We mistakenly believe we have to control everything instead of surrendering to God's will. Yes, we need to complete a myriad of daily tasks at home—we have a life to lead here; but in the moments that things do not go as planned, consider what God may be revealing through life's unexpected twists.

Thoughts to Consider

❖ When the unexpected happens, ask yourself, "Could there be a lesson here?"

❖ Instead of trying to assert control over events that feel they are spiraling away from you, think, "How am I reacting?" and, "Is this what He wants me to be aware of?"

❖ Consider how His love is being revealed in every circumstance, good and bad.

LOST IN LOVE

YOU CANNOT MAKE SOMEONE LOVE YOU. ALL you can do is become someone who can be loved. The rest is up to the other person. Love is what happens to you when you are absorbed to the point that you forget yourself and merge with the object of your attention. In an intense love affair our thoughts are only of the beloved. We can lose all appetite for food and awareness of the passage of time. We become as one with the focus of our attention. If we make God our focus we lose ourselves in Him. And when we focus on love we become love.

"Love: That is a true experience of what God is like. Every experience of human love is an instrument we can use to explore the mystery of God. Friendships, attractions, they all have their part to play and are hints of God saying, 'You love that person? You are only drawn to that person because you are drawn to me.' All that is lovable has its origin in him who is the most lovable of all."

CARDINAL BASIL HUME

SHARING THE INTENSITY

WE GENERALLY BECOME AWARE OF LOVE ONLY in fleeting moments: on seeing the smile of a child, hearing uplifting music, watching light dance on wet leaves following rain, when the heart skips a beat at the thought of a dear one. Some individuals can feel happy for no obvious reason at all; others experience love at its closest when they feel sad. God is love, and our sense of love may be evoked by any intense states of feeling. These are the special moments, but the feelings they evoke are just a sample of the unlimited love that is with us all the time. Whenever you experience love do not hoard it; allow it to flow through you to the next person you meet. Be a part of the divine love that surrounds and penetrates us all. Love is at its most vibrant when it is shared.

"One way to begin cultivating this ability to love is to see yourself internally as a center of love, as an oasis of peace, as a pool of serenity with ripples going out to all those around you."

DESMOND TUTU WITH DOUGLAS ADAMS

FALLING IN LOVE WITH GOD

MAKE A RELATIONSHIP WITH GOD IN YOUR heart. At first you may forget He is there, but as you develop the habit of turning inward to converse with Him (in the silence of your thoughts), a relationship will develop. Fake it until you make it, if you like. For any relationship to develop we first hang out together for a while, allowing love to grow, if it will. It cannot be rushed. By spending quality time contemplating God we give love a chance. An inner friendship warms to love as we feel we draw nearer to Him. The veils drop one by one until we arrive at a sense of the divine presence within, and know He is with us. He was always near, just waiting for us to get acquainted. If necessary, make a conscious effort to turn your mind inward to be with Him in this way until the real desire to be with Him replaces the need for imitation. Then, instead of a social ritual of Sunday church-going followed by a week in which you do not spare Him a thought, you develop an intimate relationship with God and He is with you at all times. You become aware of His love for you, for God loves you more than anyone else could possibly love you—more than you love yourself. Take a moment to absorb this fact. Make, every day, opportunities to show your love through the life choices you make, even if only by undertaking small acts of generosity and kindness. Your everyday life reveals the extent of your love.

ARE YOU READY TO LOVE?
A Questionnaire

THE QUESTIONS SET OUT ON THE PAGES that follow help reveal your expectations and general approach to love, life, and other people. These expectations may dictate your ability to love and be loved. There are no right or wrong answers here; use a separate piece of paper to write down your thoughts to each question, then take some time to ponder the picture they build up. Consider how your answers reflect the way in which you think and behave, and muse on what you might like to change.

- Have you ever been passionately in love? Try to recall the thoughts and sensations you experienced then, and let yourself bathe in them for a while.

- Do you love yourself?

- Does God intend us to love one another?

- What would you not do for one you love?

- Are you aware of God's love in nature and other people?

- Do you deserve to love and be loved?

- Who would be pleased to see you in love?

⊕ Who would be irritated if you were in love, and why?

⊕ Would you feel disloyal if you showed love to someone who has let you down?

⊕ If someone expresses love for you in word or deed, do you automatically look for reasons why it will not last, cannot be as good as it seems, or is bound to end badly?

⊕ Are you less comfortable with love than with criticism?

⊕ Do you believe friendships depend on a sharing of miseries?

- Were you hurt and angry so often in the past that you became more comfortable with cynicism and distrust than with praise and love?

- Do material acquisitions or food compensate for unhappiness?

- Are you suspicious or afraid when love is expressed to you?

- Is love only to be expected in another life, never in this one?

- Are you afraid to forgive?

- If you decide not to grant forgiveness, could anyone else do it on your behalf? How would this help you?

❀ Would you feel disloyal, to yourself or others, if by forgiving a wrongdoer you were freed from bitterness?

❀ Who would be pleased to see you happy, and how does that make you feel?

❀ Who would be irritated if you were happy, and why?

❀ Can you forgive someone today? Be completely honest in your answer.

❀ Are you afraid to love?

❀ In childhood did you feel loved and appreciated for yourself, despite any childish faults or misdemeanors?

- Is any child born without the capacity for love?

- Do you believe suffering to be a necessary part of life?

- Do you expect to love again at some future time? If so, what will have changed between now and then to make that possible?

- Is love impossible now?

- Have you told anyone you love him or her today?

PART 2

How to Start Loving

TO HAVE A LOVE OF GOD AND A LOVE for each other are the two great Christian injunctions. If you are looking for love, start by giving love in a myriad ways every day. Give, and give, and give. The more love and compassion you put out, the more love will blossom in your life. This chapter contains some practical plans to start you loving.

SMALL ACTS OF KINDNESS

MAKE EACH DAY AN OPPORTUNITY TO SHOW your love by extending acts of kindness toward each person you meet. Be willing to be the one who makes the kind gesture and says the compassionate word, rather than holding back for fear of looking foolish or being rejected. Once you are intent on giving rather than getting, you will find your focus shifts from what people might say or think, and so if someone's reaction to your kind word is a rebuttal, it is of no importance. Perhaps they have not yet opened their heart to receive love.

"Works of love are always works of peace. Whenever you share love with others, you'll notice the peace that comes to you and to them. When there is peace, there is God—and that is how God touches our lives and shows His love for us by pouring peace and joy into our hearts..."

MOTHER TERESA

LOVE IN ACTION

LOVE IS IN THE DETAIL. THE DISCREET OFFER of help to a neighbor who needs it. A pie delivered to a family in trouble or with a newborn baby and no time to cook; an offer to look after a family's pets when they have to attend an out-of-state wedding or be at the bedside of a sick relative; even the offer to clean shoes the day before a funeral can be of immense practical support. To stop and exchange everyday pleasantries with the mother of a child who is in trouble with the police can be a welcome act of love at a time when she fears she will be shunned by neighbors. Small charitable acts such as these can make such a difference to someone facing tough challenges. They convey more than practical help alone. They convey God's compassion and love—through you. Put yourself in another person's shoes and it is not hard to think up ways to express God's love in action. There need be no mention of religious intent. It is in the modest acts of love that we shall be known by God, not in forcing religious opinions upon individuals in a vulnerable state. Actions speak louder than words.

"Love is a verb."

ANON

The Pharisee and
the Publican

"Two men went up into the temple to pray; the one a Pharisee, and the other a publican. The Pharisee stood and prayed thus with himself, God, I thank thee, that I am not as other men are, extortioners, unjust, adulterers, or even as this publican. I fast twice in the week, I give tithes of all that I possess. And the publican, standing afar off, would not lift up so much as his eyes unto heaven, but smote upon his breast, saying, God be merciful to me a sinner. I tell you, this man went down to his house justified rather than the other: for every one that exalteth himself shall be abased; and he that humbleth himself shall be exalted."

THE GOSPEL OF ST. LUKE 18:10–14

ANALYZING THE STORY

THE PHARISEE WHO PRAYED SILENTLY, YET WAS proud of his generosity and pious acts, believing they made him better than other people, did not impress Jesus. It was the publican who berated himself as a sinner though he had genuine longing and faith, who touched Jesus. (Pharisees were strict observers of religious law with much public show but questionable sincerity, whereas publicans, as tax gatherers for the Romans, were generally considered contemptible). God knows the content of your heart. He is not fooled by appearances.

"We need heralds of the Gospel
Who are experts in humanity,
Who know the depths of the human heart,
Who can share the joys, the hopes,
The agonies, the distress of people today,
But who are, at the same time,
Contemplatives who have fallen
in love with God."

POPE JOHN PAUL II

OPEN YOUR HEART

WE WERE ALL BORN INNOCENT, TRUSTING AND loving, but modern life can so dent and bruise trust that we learn to close off our emotional needs. Sadly, when we start to expect that love will not come our way, we defend our vulnerability and deny our need to share love. Defense can become a habit, accompanied by a habitual rebuttal of any compliments or kindness directed toward us. Acknowledging love when it comes our way can help to open that closed heart and so it exposes us to renewed risk of pain. A common response is to pretend, even to ourselves, that we don't want love. This brittle veneer of self-sufficiency and denial of a need for love is just a protective mask; and, as such, may drop when exposed to continuous love, kindness, and understanding. We all have a deep desire to believe that any love offered us is real, but if past hurts have been great, this urge may be buried deep within the unconscious mind. Happily, the greater the emotional defenses, the greater the need for love. So don't be put off if your kindnesses are not always welcomed and reciprocated. You may be sure they are getting through that emotional armor, even if a response is not immediately forthcoming.

WELCOME LOVE IN

HOW ABOUT YOU? ARE YOU PREPARED TO accept love when someone is kind, generous, or compassionate toward you? Love flows naturally when it is sincere and extended without a selfish motive. The world we live in is united by God's love. It's the web that links us all beneath our conscious, ego-driven selves. There is a part, however deeply buried, in each of us that knows this and yearns to risk giving and receiving love. Christ asked this of us above all else: that we love one another. If we take no other part of his teaching than this, and live it, we are doing God's will and fulfiling our purpose on earth. Through loving human exchanges we gain glimpses of God's purpose.

"God has created me to do him some definite service; he has committed some work to me which he has not committed to another. I have my mission—I may never know it in this life, but I shall be told it in the next. I am a link in a chain, a bond of connection between persons. He has not created me for nought. I shall do good. I shall do his work.."

CARDINAL NEWMAN

KEEP AWAKE

BE AWAKE TO HIS SIGNS IN THE EVERYDAY events you encounter. Consider in all things what God might be showing you. Is it that you are loved? That you matter to Him? Perhaps it's a reminder of how not to behave when you notice someone's mean words or deeds, or recognize how negative you were when you behaved similarly. Teaching is the act of a caring Father. The sense we have within us of right and wrong springs from His love. Every person and event we encounter—those we enjoy and those we prefer to avoid—are vehicles for understanding God's message. When we are aware of Him in all things we draw nearer to Him and can draw solace from Him.

"...You must surrender all other love for His love, for Jesus desires to be loved alone, and above all things. The love of creatures is deceptive and unstable; the love of Jesus is faithful and enduring. Whoever clings to any creature will fall with its falling; but he who holds to Jesus shall stand firm for ever. Love him, therefore, and keep Him as your friend; for when all others desert you, he will not abandon you, nor allow you to perish at the last. ...Hold fast to Jesus, both in life and death, and trust yourself to his faithfulness, for he alone can aid you when all others fail"

THOMAS À KEMPIS

FIND THE GOOD IN THE BAD

CAN YOU GET IN TOUCH WITH THE LOVE BEHIND every experience? It may not be obvious when the experience, on first impressions, seems purely negative. But, on reflection, we can detect the love present even in angry words—in the concern and wisdom we know lies beneath them, for instance. Just as much love can be inspired by this as by a beautiful flower. God's presence can be felt in a sick room or at a dear one's passing. He is at the trauma room and memorial service in a kind gesture, the touch of a hand, a smile. Perhaps He is showing that you have greater fortitude and powers of endurance than you suspected you were capable of. Sometimes we need to step back from the immediate emotional experience to sense the bigger picture and understand that every event is a gift from a loving God. Death may be a healing for the person who passes when life has become continual suffering. Sickness may be a valuable lesson that prompts us to make life changes. A terrorist act can unite peoples in grief and the will to overcome. A natural disaster brings forth generosity, and engenders community spirit among rescuers and caregivers, united in their loving effort to help. Birth is a joy to be celebrated even if we cannot imagine where we will find the resources to cope or the timing could have suited us better. This illness, this baby, this grief may be a lesson tailored just for you.

ACT LIKE JESUS

HOW THEN SHOULD WE SHOW OUR LOVE as Jesus did? By giving freely of our time and support to others. By offering practical help without expecting recognition or thanks. By having compassion for those less fortunate than ourselves because of bad luck or circumstance. By forgiving those who are better off than we are (who teach us about envy and jealousy, or generosity and philanthropy). By extending forgiveness to those who are truly penitent and those who are not, for all sinners are God's children. We must be humble, ready to admit our wrongs and not too proud to tackle what-

ever work God presents for us to do. At times
we may need to be heroic, to fight for what is
right or to defend the weak, for love is action,
not a theoretical stance. Love demands everything from us, and yet by sharing out our love
we experience love. That is the paradox. To get
it we must give it away.

*"God is everywhere, in everything. When
you see something beautiful—a sunset, a
mountain, a stream—these are reminders
of God's presence, revealing his beauty."*

CARDINAL BASIL HUME

"Love is watchful, and while resting, never sleeps; weary, it is never exhausted; imprisoned, it is never in bonds; alarmed, it is never afraid; like a living flame and a burning torch, it surges upward and surely surmounts every obstacle. Whoever loves God knows well the sound of His voice. A loud cry in the ears of God is that burning love of the soul which exclaims, 'my God and my love, you are all mine, and I am all Yours."

THOMAS À KEMPIS

"For God so loved the world, that he gave his only begotten Son, that whosoever believeth in him should not perish, but have everlasting life."

THE GOSPEL OF ST. JOHN 3:16

START TODAY

IT IS WHAT YOU DO WITH TODAY THAT MATTERS. Make every day a chance to show your love, even if only in small acts of generosity. Put the needs of others first. Allow another person to go before you at the supermarket checkout, especially if he or she is frail, elderly, or has only a few items. Give up a seat on public transport to someone less able to stand than you. Do you recall the "Practice Random Acts Of Kindness And Senseless Beauty" movement in the U.S.A.? People passing through tollgates on highways paid their own fee plus another toll for whoever might follow next, though who that might be was unknown to the benefactor. The craze spread, with people leaving theater tickets at the box office for the next in line, creating ripples of happiness while it lasted. How much more worthwhile is such trusting generosity than taking every petty opportunity to cheat or defraud? Mean acts leave cheater more diminished than cheated. Be generous with your acts of kindness. Jesus tells us that what we do for another person we do for Him. Imagine everyone you meet is Jesus in disguise. Would you behave differently toward them? Jesus showed by example that He loves us all equally and unconditionally. If you would like to be loved like that, why not begin by practicing it yourself, starting today? Could showing love be such a sacrifice?

"Love is a mighty power, a great and complete good; Love alone lightens every burden, and makes the rough places smooth. It bears every hardship as though it were nothing, and renders all bitterness sweet and acceptable. The love of Jesus is noble, and inspires us to great deeds; it moves us always to desire perfection. Love aspires to high things, and is held back by nothing base. Love longs to be free, a stranger to every worldly desire, lest its inner vision become dimmed, and lest worldly self-interest hinder it or ill-fortune cast it down. Nothing is sweeter than love, nothing stronger, nothing higher, nothing wider, nothing

*more pleasant, nothing fuller or better
in heaven or earth; for love is born of
God, and can rest only in God,
above all created things.
Love flies, runs, and leaps with joy;
it is free and unrestrained. Love gives
all for all, resting in One who flows and
proceeds. Love does not regard the gifts,
but turns to the Giver of all good gifts.
Love knows no limits, but ardently
transcends all bounds. Love feels no
burden, takes no account of toil, attempts
things beyond its strength; love sees
nothing as impossible, for it feels able to
achieve all things. Love therefore does
great things; it is strange and effective;
while he who lacks love faints and fails."*

THOMAS À KEMPIS

71

PRAYERS, POEMS,

and

THOUGHTS

of

LOVE

"Teach me, my God and King,
In all things Thee to see,
And what I do in anything,
To do it as for Thee."

GEORGE HERBERT

"When you know how much God is in love with you then you can only live your life radiating that love."

MOTHER TERESA

"Love all God's creation—the whole of it... love every leaf, every ray of light. Love the animals, love the plants, love everything. If you love everything, you will perceive the mystery of God in all... you will come at last to love the whole world with an all-embracing love."

FYODR DOSTOEVSKY

"God bless all those that I love;
God bless all those that love me;
God bless all those that love those that
I love and all those that love those that
love me. Amen."

EMBROIDERED ON A SIXTEENTH/SEVENTEENTH
CENTURY SAMPLER

"O most merciful Redeemer,
Friend, and Brother,
May we know Thee more clearly,
Love thee more dearly,
Follow thee more nearly;
For ever and ever. Amen."

ST. RICHARD OF CHICHESTER

"That best portion of a good man's life,
His little, nameless, unremembered acts
Of kindness and love."

WILLIAM WORDSWORTH

"God showed me in my palm ❖
A little thing round as a ball ❖
About the size of a hazelnut. ❖
I looked at it with the eye of my
understanding ❖ And asked
myself: ❖ 'What is this thing?'
❖ And I was answered: 'It is
everything that is created.' ❖

I wondered how it could survive since it seemed so little ❖ *It could suddenly disintegrate into nothing.* ❖ *The answer came: 'It endures and ever will endure,* ❖ *Because God loves it.'* ❖ *And so everything has being because of God's love."*

JULIAN OF NORWICH

PART 3

Surrendering to Love

THE KINGDOM OF LOVE ON EARTH shall come about when humanity is as one family in which all sisters and brothers are beloved by their Holy Father. This kingdom will come only when enough of us accept the need for divine love and God's forgiveness with true humility. The meek shall inherit the earth, the meek being those humble enough to submit to God's will, rather than the dictates of a selfish ego. God gives us freewill in order that the decision to accept Him as our Lord is one we make from choice.

FROM THE HEART

GOD LOVES US AND WANTS US TO RETURN TO Him, but we humans have freewill. Freewill offers each of us a wonderful playground to explore; it is within this playground that we come to realize our love of God and our need to return to the source. Here, we learn to love God because we do, not because we are ordered to. If we make a great show of religious zeal yet have an impure heart, like the proud Pharisee, we show no humility and God is not deceived, since He is with each of us at all times. If, however, we are like the reviled publican whose heart was sincere, and faith humble and modest, God welcomes us into the kingdom of love. The first shall be last and the last shall be first. It may be that a wife shall be included and a husband not, or vice versa. Earthly associations are of no relevance when the sincerity of the heart is in question, as Luke tells us in chapter 17, verses 20–37.

"And when he was demanded of the Pharisees, when the kingdom of God should come, he answered them and said, 'The kingdom of God cometh not with observation: Neither shall they say, Lo here! or, lo there! for, behold, the kingdom of God is within you."

THE GOSPEL OF ST. LUKE 17: 20–21

GIVING UP THE BLING

MONEY AND POSSESSIONS ARE NOT BAD IN themselves, but when we value them above love and each other, we lose our way. We sell ourselves cheap when we choose attachment to transient goods—that Rolex watch, those Gucci shoes, the bottle of Cristal—over eternal love. Unless we become as innocent as a little child, trusting completely, loving, and surrendering to greater authority, we exclude ourselves from God's kingdom. Material compensation instead of God's love? We all have the freedom to choose.

"When we take an extra step or walk an extra mile, we do so in opposition to the inertia of laziness or the resistance of fear. Moving out against laziness we call work; moving out in the face of fear we call courage, Love, then, is a form of work or a form of courage. Since it requires the extension of ourselves, love is always either work or courage. If an act is not one of work or courage, then it is not an act of love. There are no exceptions."

M. SCOTT PECK

GETTING DOWN AND DIRTY

WHEN JESUS AND HIS DISCIPLES MET FOR their last supper together, they found no slave present to wash their feet, as was customary in that era before entering a room in which food would be served. Foot washing is not the most pleasant of tasks and normally would be the job of a slave, but as there was no slave present, Jesus poured water into a basin and started to clean his disciples's feet himself. Simon Peter was horrified at the thought of his beloved teacher performing such a lowly task upon him, and protested, but Jesus told him that unless he allowed him to perform this humble duty, Simon Peter could not be counted as one of Jesus' followers. In making ourselves truly humble before others and getting down to unpleasant tasks without complaint, we follow Christ's example of perfect love in action.

"Verily, verily, I say unto you, The servant is not greater than his lord, neither he that is sent greater than he that sent him. If ye know these things, happy are ye if ye do them."

THE GOSPEL OF ST. JOHN 13:16–17

Jesus Washes His Disciples's Feet

"Now before the feast of the passover, when Jesus knew that his hour was come that he should depart out of this world unto the Father, having loved his own which were in the world, he loved them unto the end. And supper being ended, the devil having now put into the heart of Judus Iscariot, Simon's son, to betray him; Jesus knowing that the Father had given all things into his hands, and that he

was come from God, and went to God;
He riseth from supper, and laid aside
his garments; and took a towel,
and girded himself.
After that he poureth water into a bason,
and began to wash the disciples' feet,
and to wipe them with the towel
wherewith he was girded.
Then cometh he unto Simon Peter:
and Peter saith unto him, Lord,
dost thou wash my feet?
Jesus answered and said unto him,
What I do thou knowest not now;
but thou shalt know hereafter.
Peter saith unto him, Thou shalt never
wash my feet. Jesus answered him,
If I wash thee not, thou hast
no part with me."

THE GOSPEL OF ST. JOHN 13:1–8

ANALYZING THE STORY

JESUS EXPLAINS TO SIMON PETER THAT THE Savior comes to cleanse our sins, and that if we deny his humility, we refuse both him and his message. Thus the cleansing of feet at the last supper is a metaphor for cleansing Simon Peter's soul: If he rejects the gesture, he rejects also the substance. Later in the last supper, Jesus uses more metaphors to teach his disciples—the breaking of bread and drinking of wine. They are encouraged to share the blood (wine) and body (bread) of Christ the Savior, consuming them in remembrance of Him. And so in the act of remembering Him as they perform this ritual in future (during each Holy Communion), they have a metaphor for Christ's forgiveness and His self-sacrifice for their sins. (Read the entire episode in John 13:1–30.) Jesus commands the disciples to do as he has done, to humbly confess their sins and to accept the sacrifices thrust upon them as a mark of their commitment. They must forgive and accept each other, and all whom they meet, as Jesus has taught them and showed them. We all learn from this story.

"If I then, your Lord and master, have washed your feet; ye also ought to wash one another's feet.
For I have given you an example, that ye should do as I have done to you."

THE GOSPEL OF ST. JOHN 13:13–15

"My little children, let us not love in word, neither in tongue; but in deed and in truth. ❧ And hereby we know that we are of the truth, and shall assure our hearts before him. ❧ For if our heart condemn us, God is greater than our heart, and knoweth all things. ❧ Beloved, if our heart condemn us not, then we have confidence toward God. ❧ And whatsoever we ask, we receiveth him because

we keep his commandments, and do those things that are pleasing in his sight. ✧ And this is his commandment, That we should believe on the name of his son Jesus Christ, and love one another, as he gave us commandment. ✧ And he that keepeth his commandments dwelleth in him, and he in him. And hereby we know that he abideth in us, by the spirit which he hath given us."

1 JOHN 3: 18–24

TRUSTING IN LOVE

WE TRUST THOSE WE LOVE, BUT AT TIMES IT CAN seem as if God has forsaken us; that he is not aware of the difficulties we are facing. This is when our love is tested. It's easy to place our trust in Him when life is going our way. But how easy is it when all seems lost? It is only when things become difficult that our trust and love for God are really tested. Can you accept that everything is God's will, even when you do not like the way things are turning out? If you can still place your trust in him even when you feel forsaken, that is a measure of your love. To do so, despite having no sense of His presence, is proof that you trust in God's will, because you continue to pray even when you receive no obvious benefit. To pray at such times shows an intent to please God and not ourselves. And when His nearness steals over us, we shall know it stems from His grace, not our will.

"Trusting God when things are not clear is one of the hardest things to do but one of the greatest marks of our love."

CARDINAL BASIL HUME

"... Once you love a person, then you grow in the knowledge of them. That is what faith is like, the beginning of a love story. The more you get involved then the more you begin to trust.."

CARDINAL BASIL HUME

A POPE'S STORY

ANGELO RONCALLI FROM SOTTO IL MONTE, A village in Northern Italy, became Pope John 23rd in 1958. He wrote the following words on the merits and the difficulties of placing trust in God in his opening address to the Second Vatican Council in 1962:

"When I left Sotto il Monte to go to the seminary, I found that the seminary was cold and the food was bad, and I was rather miserable. I said to myself, 'Angelo, this is no place for you.' But then I thought, 'God brought me here

*and I must trust him.' So I stayed and
I was ordained a priest. Then I became
a bishop's secretary. I carried the bishop's
bags and I drove him round and I did
this and I did that. And, occasionally,
I would say to myself, 'Angelo, this is no
place for you.' But then I thought,
'God has brought me here and I must
trust him.' Then I was drafted into the
Vatican diplomatic service and I was
sent to Bulgaria! I used to receive letters
from the secretariat of State telling me
whom to see, and what to say, and where
to go. And I would write back telling
them who I had seen, what I had said,
and where I had gone. It was all very
mundane and I used to say to myself,
'Angelo, this is no place for you.'
But then I reflected that God had*

brought me there and I trusted him. Then I became cardinal patriarch of Venice and I was very happy. In 1958 Pope Pius 12th died and, at the age of 77, I went to Rome for the Conclave. And I said to myself, 'Angelo, they wouldn't, would they?' But they did! So here I am, surrounded by cardinals, archbishops, and monsignori, all preventing me from doing what I would like to do, which is go out for a meal to have a chat with my family. But God brought me where I am and I trust him. In his providence he has brought you where you are and we must all trust him."

POPE JOHN XXIII

"In the garden of Gethsemane the night before his arrest, Jesus prayed to his heavenly Father to spare him the ordeal he knew he faced, but added that his Father should do so only if it be His will. Even at the point of humiliation, torture, and death, Jesus shows his love and trust in the Lord and a willingness to accept and suffer all for Him. Sometimes it is in accepting the things we cannot change that we show our love and trust. However bad a situation may seem, Christians know God's love will prevail."

THE GOSPEL OF ST. MARK 14:32–36

"And he went forward a little, and fell on the ground, and prayed that, if it were possible, the hour might pass from him. And he said, Abba, Father, all things are possible unto thee; take away this cup from me: nevertheless not what I will, but what thou wilt."

MARK: 14: 35–36

PRAYERS, POEMS,

and

THOUGHTS

of

LOVE

"This is my commandment, that ye love one another as I have loved you."

THE GOSPEL OF ST. JOHN 15:12

"Most loving Lord, give me a childlike love of Thee, which may cast out all fear. Amen."

E.B.PUDSEY

"What can I give Him,
Poor as I am?
If I were a shepherd
I would bring a lamb;
If I were a wise man
I would do my part,
Yet what can I give Him?
Give my heart."

CHRISTINA ROSSETTI

"Thou, my God, who art Love, art Love that loveth, and Love that is loveable, and Love that is the bond between these twain."

NICOLAS OF CUSA

"Love seeks no cause beyond itself and no fruit; it is its own fruit, its own I love because I love; I love in order that I may love."

ST. BERNARD

"How sweet it is to love, and to be dissolved, and as it were to bathe myself in thy love."

THOMAS À KEMPIS

"Love cannot distrust."

MEISTER ECKHART

"[Divine love] is a love that clothes us, enfolds and embraces us and... completely surrounds us, never to leave us."

"O Lord our God, grant us grace to desire you with our whole heart, that so desiring we may seek and find you and so finding you, may love you, and so loving you, may hate those sins from which you have redeemed us. Amen."

ST ANSELM

"Love divine, all loves excelling
Joy heaven, to earth come down,
Fix in us thy humble dwelling
All thy faith full mercies crown.
Jesus thou art all compassion,
Pure unbounded love thou art;
Visit us with thy salvation,
Enter every trembling heart."

CHARLES WESLEY

PART 4

Love and Marriage

HEN A COUPLE CONTRACTS TO marry through the exchange of vows, God recognizes in their union a commitment that mirrors the love Christ has for all who would follow him. In marriage, partners commit to love and cherish each other come what may, through sickness or health, in wealth or poverty, until death shall part them. If the marriage is blessed with children we gain more opportunities to share and express love.

DARING TO DATE

AS WITH LEARNING TO RIDE A BICYCLE, SPEAK A new language, or attempt any new endeavor, learning to form an intimate loving relationship with a partner takes practice. There will be trials and some errors, because if we never risk getting it wrong, we will never get it right. The process is similar to acquiring any new skill: We have some idea of the behavior required, then try it out, make mistakes, try again, and in the process refine what we know about the subject and ourselves. In the business of establishing loving relationships, the tricky part is that unlike learning a new language or how to swim, our test subject will also be trying out what he or she knows about love, too. Reassure yourself with the thought that both of you share a desire for the relationship to go well. To risk the embarrassment of rejection takes courage, so if you have got as far as a date with a possible suitor, both parties are likely to have already made as many preliminary assessments of compatibility as were possible. If you are nervous, as is likely, remember, it is likely your date is too.

THE PERFECT EXAMPLE

LEARNING TO LOVE CAN BE A SCARY PROSPECT, but we have the best role model imaginable for offering and getting back love in exchange in the life of Jesus. He shows us how to give and receive love without expectations and regardless of personal cost. Whatever you've learnt about giving and receiving love from your family on earth makes no difference; you have in God the perfect Father, whose love for you is always non-judgmental, who is ever present to your needs, and who knows your deepest secrets, yet still loves you. Know that you are as worthy and deserving of love and happiness as any other being. You are so much more than your fears, mistakes, and self-doubt. We are all surrounded by and constantly immersed in love, though we may choose to believe otherwise. It is we who turn our faces away, seduced to look elsewhere by a busy life or stressful events. We can choose to turn back to the light within us at any time. It was never diminished. Turn within, to God's love, and you will find it easy to find love outside.

> *"You may not be in love with God, but God is most certainly in love with you. Always remember that."*
>
> CARDINAL BASIL HUME

ON LOVE AND REJECTION

SOMETIMES YOU MAY KNOW YOU ARE LOVED by another person, but can't reciprocate the affection. Don't feel ashamed, and don't allow feelings of shame to ripen into anger because shame is such an uncomfortable emotion. To reject another person is always difficult, especially when you know you are loved. Remember that you are not the author of someone else's emotions. How anyone else feels is their responsibility, but how you reciprocate is yours. This is not to suggest you deny your own truth. So long as your dealings are decent, truthful, and considerate while maintaining your individual rights, rejection need not be an assault on the other person's personality. A disappointment, perhaps, but just an honest expression, lovingly handled.

"You can't live provisionally and you can't love provisionally."

POPE JOHN PAUL II

JOINING TOGETHER

THE LOVE OF HUSBAND AND WIFE IS A REFLECTION of divine love. Through this match on earth we get to experience firsthand—through body, mind, and emotions—the transforming nature of heartfelt passion, devotion, and commitment, and the way that this special sacrament enriches and strengthens each partner while bringing them together as "one flesh." We should be aware that the selfless, unconditional married love commended through holy scripture signifies the mystery of the union between Christ and his Church and is but a dim reflection of God's eternal love for us. Marriage doesn't just glorify the couple who exchange vows. The words of the wedding ceremony reveal how a marriage enables the dissemination of love on a more widespread scale. The prayers after the exchange of rings urge us to "reach out in love and concern for others," for marriage brings with it such fulfilment of mutual affection that it allows each partner to spread a little of the faithfulness, patience, peace, and honor that exemplify the love that Jesus Christ lived.

> *"Love grows by means of truth and the truth draws near to man by means of love."*
>
> POPE JOHN PAUL II

FOR EVER AND EVER?

ON YOUR WEDDING DAY, YOUR HOPE AND BELIEF is that this union will last forever. But we live in the twenty-first century, when it is impossible not to know that a back door exists (in the form of divorce). In an era of serial marriages, all too often bonds of commitment are adapted to suit convenience. Couples enter into wedlock in the knowledge that they can back out later if their taste changes, a partner stops being attractive, or fails to provide the material or emotional comforts they have decided they must have.

"...With our spouse, we don't always feel loving and romantic. If married life depended on our feelings for our spouse from moment to moment, very, very, few would survive. True love is when you are feeling as dead as a stone and you say to yourself, "This is the one to whom I have committed myself and she has committed herself to me." You do not have a great deal of control over when you feel resentful or irritable, but you can still choose to be loving—to act lovingly. Sometimes the best you can do is say to God or to yourself, I want to love. Sometimes the best you can do is to say, I want to want to love."

DESMOND TUTU WITH DOUGLAS ADAMS

127

Questions to Ponder

❋ How would you feel if you went about life in the knowledge that God has a back door he might use to release Him from His commitment toward us? Take a moment to explore the emotions this calls up.

❋ Does the world you picture when you consider this idea seem a radically different and more frightening place?

◈ Can you now see just how important it is to be aware that God loves each of us unconditionally?

◈ Do you now have a better understanding of the value real commitment brings to a relationship, whether of the flesh or of the spirit?

"Jesus calls his followers to love one another as he loves them; not just to love others as one loves oneself. He proposes something new; to love others with the very love of God; to see them with the eyes of the Lord. And we can only see

and love them like that if we have experienced Jesus loving us with a liberating love. It is only then that we can open ourselves and become vulnerable and grow into greater openness to others."

JEAN VANIER

KEEPING LOVE STRONG

NEVER PART FROM YOUR LOVED ONE WITH CROSS words—the unexpected waits around every corner. How sad if the last words you exchanged in this life were bitter ones. No slight or disagreement between loved ones was ever intended to be irrevocable. Be careful that yours are not. To those who really love each other, occasional disagreements happen, but are just ripples on the surface of deeper water, and both partners are secure in the knowledge of this. The loving couple always makes up their differences because their bond is more valuable than proving a point.

"By the power of your Holy Spirit, pour out the abundance of your blessing upon this man and this woman. Lead them into all peace. Let their love for each other be a seal upon their hearts, a mantle about their shoulders, and a crown upon their foreheads."

THE BOOK OF COMMON PRAYER (1928)

FAMILY LOVE

THE LOVE WE EXPERIENCE AS INFANTS AND children shapes the lives we lead as adults. God is love, so wherever we find love—within or without—we find God. The family is the crucible of emotional experiences, so, for most of us, our first experience of love occurs in a family setting. It's here that we first explore loving relationships—with our parents, siblings, cousins and grandparents—and it is this model of love we draw on when we go on to form intimate relationships and then loving partnerships as adults. And so, when a family practices Christian values in the home, these loving values are carried over into the school and workplace, the neighborhood and seat of government, and, eventually, into every part of society, for what is society but the biggest of families? As we believe, so we behave.

"...Love begins at home and that is why it is important to pray together. If you pray together you will stay together and love each other as God loves each one of you.."

MOTHER TERESA

LOVE IS...

THE BOND BETWEEN MOST PARENTS AND THEIR children is without preconditions. Love simply is—from the moment of birth to the grave. There is no, "I will only love you if..." between parent and child, though some parents find they express love through actions rather than words. They might feel they have to maintain an appearance of authority, for instance, or might find it difficult to talk of love to anyone, even to the children they adore. The sacrifices a parent makes for a child, in time, lost sleep, and hard cash, for instance, are an expression of love as loud as any proclamation. In the family, we fondly overlook character flaws in those we love as mere aspects of a personality. We are willing to sacrifice our own desires and plans to provide for our children, and want only the best for them. We will move mountains to help them if they are in trouble and will fight their battles for them, if they will allow it. Such is the all-embracing love God has for us, as Jesus tells us throughout the gospels.

"If there is room in the heart there is room in the house."

DANISH PROVERB

FAMILIES AT WAR

PARADOXICALLY, THOUGH FAMILY LIFE AFFORDS us great opportunities to give and receive love, it can also be a war zone. The members of an inharmonious family may find the intensity of differing emotional needs leads to arguments and fights. As a wit once put it, we choose our friends but are stuck with our families. While it is the center of loving relationships, family life offers scope for rivalry and irritation between members who know each other beyond all pretence. There can be no airs and graces and not many convincing deceits. Family squabbles are usually less serious than they sound. Bickering can be a way of expressing love, for some people. Like noisy starlings—those birds that seem endlessly to squabble and squawk yet have a strong team spirit—we often test other family members more than we might dare test strangers, because we know we love and are loved by them, however our family feuds look or sound to outsiders. So when people argue, it doesn't mean they don't love each other. Sadly, the opposite is also true; it doesn't mean they love each other if they never argue. There are many ways to show love.

"No bird soars too high, if he soars with his own wings."

WILLIAM BLAKE

DOES LOVE HAVE BOUNDARIES?

LEARNING HOW TO BECOME AN ADULT REQUIRES that we test our fledgling individualism against resistance. The family is generally the chosen arena because the degrees of risk are better known, and any failures less demoralizing. Most children test their ability to resist authority and learn how to exercise personal power within the known confines of the family in which they are loved. It feels safer than expressing such risky feelings among strangers or less intimate acquaintances. They can try on ideas for size, strike attitudes, assume opinions, acquire manners and social principles, learn how to say 'No,' when appropriate, and formulate individual codes of conduct in an arena where to push the boundaries will not have disastrous consequences. The guidance of loving adults who have clear moral values and understand the need for resistance as a necessary part of becoming an individual is the best template for the child shaping its own ethical position. Love that allows exploration within safe boundaries achieves more than tyrannical insistence on a fearful obedience.

WHERE LOVE IS LACKING

SOME PEOPLE LOVE US DEARLY BUT JUST DON'T know how to show it. Unfortunately, the effects of growing up in the absence of love can pass from generation to generation. Some parents are so damaged they are incapable of finding love within themselves, recognizing it outside themselves, and giving to others what they've never known. Emotional expression may be selfish and conditional, trading guilty feelings against powerful needs, and giving rise to emotional manipulation, "Do this for me, then I will love you…" being the implied message, even if not directly stated. Love for oneself, free from bargaining or manipulation, becomes rare or non-existent. The child of a dysfunctional family learns survival tactics instead of how to give and receive love openly. With such example as the norm, dealings with others at school or as an adult may be tainted, unless life presents reasons to question the benefits. The influence of Christian contact and love can make a huge contribution to reformulating such attitudes and behavior. If your family suffered love deprivation, let it end with you. Decide to break the chain and let love, respect, compassion, tolerance, and understanding begin with you. Decide you are going to be the solution instead of an extension to the problem. Give generously of the love you longed to receive and you will be rewarded with it now. God is as present in the dysfunctional family as He is in the loving one. He is every-where; His compassion embraces all of us, whatever our situation. As a loving Father he does not interfere or take sides, loving the stern parent as much as the fearful child. But this is not to say that he is deaf to the prayers of that child. He is present in the kindly teacher or neighbor, in the resilience of the child of such a family; He shares the sorrow when there is pain to be endured. Family is in the supportive relationships; the people who love and care about us and teach us, whoever they may be. Family is not neces-sarily limited to our biological relationships.

*"And whosoever shall offend one of
these little ones that believe in me, it
is better for him that a millstone were
hanged about his neck, and he
were cast into the sea..."*

THE GOSPEL OF ST. MARK 9:42

GOD YOUR FATHER

IF YOU FEEL YOU ALWAYS MISS OUT ON LOVING relationships, think again. God's loving relationship is your birthright. His love has always been there for you, and always remains with you, though you may have been so busy looking for love elsewhere that you did not allow it to touch you. Imagine for a moment how it would be to know that you have a loving Father who wants only your happiness and wellbeing, and loves you despite your mistakes and indifference toward Him. His is a strong and warmly enveloping love that asks no questions, accepts all, rejects nothing, loves all. Just allow yourself to experience how that feels for a moment. This love was always there, but life may have caused you to pretend to be tough, to pretend you didn't want or need to be loved. Is that really true?

"Always think of God as your lover. Therefore he wants to be with you, just as a lover always wants to be with the beloved. He wants your attention as every lover wants the attention of the beloved. He wants to listen to you as every lover wants to hear the voice of the beloved. If you turn to me and ask, 'Are you in love with God?' I would pause, hesitate and say, 'I am not certain. But of one thing I am certain—that he is in love with me."

CARDINAL BASIL HUME

GUIDING OUR CHILDREN

WHEN WE RAISE OR CARE FOR CHILDREN, WE have a duty to transcend negative experiences to give the love we all would wish to receive in childhood. The children in your care learn from how you act as well as from the rules by which you instruct them. The questions set out on page 150 might help you think about the values you are passing on. We do well to look to the spiritual needs of children. They are the society of tomorrow. If they grow up in a climate of fear and hate, their ability to experience love will be severely compromised, as will our future civilization. This is an issue each of us should consider in our interactions with the young. It is not only politicians who should decide on rules of conduct and penalties for non-compliance. We are the examples shaping our future generations's young lives. If we do not like the fruit, we should take a good look at the tree. Each of us are responsible, parents or not, for providing a climate of encouragement and support, and, in our own relationships, an example of love.

"Violence occurs when we forget and deny our basic identity as God's children, when we treat one another as if we were worthless instead of priceless."

JOHN DEAR: A JESUIT PRIEST

Questions to Ponder

- ❀ Do you teach your children by example that it is possible to love and trust despite the trials life throws up?

- ❀ Are you able to rise above bitterness, fear, and mistrust of others?

- ❀ Are you an example of love conquering adversity? Remember that is not what happens to us that matters—it is how we react and what we do about it.

"For a long time it had seemed to me that life was about to begin—real life. But there was always some obstacle in the way, something to be got through first, some unfinished business, time still to be served, a debt to be paid. Then life would begin. At last it dawned on me that these obstacles were my life."

FR. ALFRED D'SOUZA

PRAYERS, POEMS,

and

THOUGHTS

of

LOVE

"*My bounty is as boundless as the sea,*
My love as deep; the more I give to thee,
The more I have, for both are infinite."

FROM *ROMEO AND JULIET*
BY WILLIAM SHAKESPEARE

"Everything that touches us, me and you,
takes us together like a violin's bow,
which draws one voice out
of two separate strings.
Upon what instrument are
we two spanned?
And what musician holds us
in his hand?"

RAINER MARIA RILKE

"Give them wisdom and devotion in the ordering of their common life, that each may be to the other a strength in need, a counselor in perplexity, a comfort in sorrow, and a companion in joy.

Grant that their wills may be so knit together in your will, and their spirits in your spirit, that they may grow in love and peace with you and with each other all the days of their life.

Give them grace, when they hurt each other, to recognize and acknowledge their fault, and to seek each other's forgiveness and yours.

Make their life together a sign of Christ's love to this suffering and broken world, that unity may overcome estrangement, forgiveness heal guilt, and joy conquer despair. Amen."

FROM THE MARRIAGE CEREMONY IN THE BOOK
OF COMMON PRAYER (1928)

"*What greater thing is there for two human souls, than to feel they are joined for life—to strengthen each other in all labour, to rest on each other in all sorrow, to minister to each other in all pain, to be one with each other in silent, unspeakable memories....*"

FROM *ADAM BEDE* BY GEORGE ELIOT

"That I may come near to her,
draw me nearer to you than to her;
that I may know her,
make me to know you more than her;
that I may love her
with the love of a perfectly whole heart,
cause me to love you more than her and
most of all."

"PRAYER BEFORE HIS MARRIAGE" BY
TEMPLE GAIRDNER

"Sensual pleasure passes and vanishes in the twinkling of an eye, but the friendship between us, the mutual confidence, the delights of the heart, the enchantment of the soul, these things do not perish and can never be destroyed."

VOLTAIRE

"You should live so that it is possible to create the kingdom of love on earth."

LEO TOLSTOY

"If a child lives with criticism, He learns to condemn, ✧ If a child lives with hostility, He learns to fight, ✧ If a child lives with ridicule, He learns to be shy, ✧ If a child lives with shame, He learns to feel guilty, ✧ If a child lives with tolerance, He learns to be patient, ✧ If a child lives with encouragement, He learns

confidence, ❖ *If a child lives with praise, He learns to appreciate,* ❖ *If a child lives with fairness, He learns justice,* ❖ *If a child lives with security, He learns to have faith,* ❖ *If a child lives with approval, He learns to like himself,* ❖ *If a child lives with acceptance and friendship, he learns to find love in the world."*

DOROTHY LAW HOLTE

PART 5

Love and Work

BRINGING LOVE INTO THE WORKPLACE has a far-reaching effect upon any organization (and I don't mean in terms of weddings and babies, though these may follow given an atmosphere of acceptance and lifted spirits). When the tenor of the working day is co-operation rather than competition, and the guiding principles ethics not sharp practice, both the individuals and the organization benefit.

LOVE IN ACTION AT WORK

TRY BEHAVING IN A LOVING MANNER TOWARD each person you meet and work with for a whole day and see how your experience of human interactions differs as a result. When the sun comes out, it lifts our spirits. When you act as if someone was worthy of your love, or as if they thought you worthy of theirs (regardless of what you would normally expect from them or for them), you bring the possibility of love into every human transaction, however professional or minor it may be, from buying a newspaper on the way to the office to your conduct in business negotiations. Your loving behavior need not be overt or outrageous—that might alienate clients or put you at risk of misinterpretation. Just try simple loving-kindness and see how it feels to express it, and how others react to it. Fake it for a while. It may not be rewarding in every case, but if you are in a spirit of giving, not getting is of no consequence.

Points to Ponder

- ◈ Were people more prone to smile than usual when you acted in this way?

- ◈ Were your interactions more positive on the whole?

- ◈ Did the day seem shorter/more pleasant?

WHY ACT LOVING AT WORK?

WE ENTER THE WORLD WITH NO POSSESSIONS and leave it the same way, but we are all born with the capacity to give and receive love. Our task as Christians is to expand our given capacity for love, taking it into every realm of life. Jesus commanded us in the New Testament to grow in our love, not just for God, but for other people; and not just for those it is easy to love, like family members and friends. God so loved every part of His creation that he sent His only son to walk among us as a practical demonstration of what it is to practice self-sacrificing, unconditional love. He showed us the way to behave in every social interaction. We are told that we are made in God's image. If we live our lives in an imitation of the love Christ showed us is possible, we may "grow in perfection, as our heavenly father is perfect." (Matthew 5:48). Aim high and share all.

> *"Prayer in action is love, and love in action is service."*
>
> MOTHER TERESA

"Whoever loves much, does much. Whoever does a thing well, does much. And he does well who serves the community before his own interests. Often an apparently loving action really springs from worldly motives; for natural inclination, self-will, hope of reward, and our own self-interest will seldom be entirely absent. ✧ *Whoever is moved by true and perfect love is never self-seeking, but desires only that God's glory may be served in all things. He*

envies none, for he seeks no plea-sures for himself, nor does he act for self-gratification, but desires above all things to merit the bless-ing of God. All good he ascribes not to men, but to God, from whom all things proceed as from their source, and in whom the Saints enjoy perfection and peace. Oh, if only a man had a spark of true love in his heart, he would know for certain that all earthly things are full of vanity."

THOMAS À KEMPIS

CHRIST'S EXAMPLE

JESUS TAUGHT US HOW TO LOVE USING STORIES of everyday life that his listeners would understand. He spoke of wayward sons, of weddings, of shepherds and their daily tasks, and other familiar situations at home and work. What was unfamiliar about Christ's teaching was the living example he set us. He showed in his daily work what it means to love without counting the cost; how to treat all as equals before God whatever their social standing, health, wealth, or other worldly attributes. He put others first even when that meant the sacrifice of his own life.

Greater love has never been known. If we would be followers of Christ, we will obey his commandment: to love one another as much as we love ourselves. When we do so, God is in us. And this godliness transforms our everyday relationships and work practices. When we face situations in which there are uncomfortable choices, we can ask, "How would Jesus have acted?" and find that we always knew the right course of action. Whether negotiating contracts or serving the public, this is a frame of mind that makes a positive difference to the daily lives of every person we encounter every day and so to wider society.

"Works of love are always a means of becoming closer to God."

MOTHER TERESA

"The extraordinary thing is that when you act lovingly you can begin to feel love. Psychologists ask, 'do we run away because we are scared, or are we scared because we are running away?' If you act for long enough in a particular way, you begin to feel the feelings that accompany the actions."

DESMOND TUTU WITH DESMOND ADAMS

GIVING AND TAKING

WE LEARN EARLY IN LIFE THAT WE ARE JUST ONE among others, and that this can give us a pleasurable experience—of being loved. But as we grow up, we quickly have to learn how to give as well as take. We cannot demand that love (or even goodwill) be shown us. It is not ours to control or demand. We also learn that when we give love (or goodwill), we are more likely to get it back in return. Look at your own professional life; can you see the same patterns at work here, too? Many of us spend time examining the health of our relationships, but fail to recognize the same themes affecting our interactions with work colleagues and clients, for good or bad. Learning to love—in a work setting as well as at home—is often as much a matter of learning to accept from others as it is of learning to give out. It is usually fear of rejection or ridicule that creates doubts and leads us to be mistrustful of love when it is offered. We all have a great capacity to express good feelings, and it is when we interact with people in a positive way (with love) that we come most fully alive.

"The greatest grace which God can give is the knowledge that he loves each one of us more than any lover ever loved his, or her, beloved. To realize that, to allow it to sink deep into our minds and hearts, can change our lives completely. Who can separate us from that love?"

CARDINAL BASIL HUME

UNIVERSAL LOVE

THROUGHOUT THE GOSPELS JESUS PROMOTES the idea of a universal society bound together by divine love. The members of this society are seen as one big family whose father is God. The old order with its multiple affiliations based on blood relations, nationhood, ethnicity, or plain self-interest will be replaced a single relationship—that of universal love between equals: a brotherhood (and sisterhood) of man. In such a society there is no resentment or jealousy. We treat each other as if we were treating ourselves, with courtesy, compassion and love.

*"[Man] created in the image of God,
shares by his work in the activity
of the Creator."*

POPE JOHN PAUL II

PRAYERS, POEMS,

and

THOUGHTS

of

LOVE

"O Lord, let us not live to be useless, for Christ's sake."

JOHN WESLEY

"Help us this day, O God, to serve thee devoutly, and the world busily. May we do our work wisely, give succour secretly, go to meat appetitely, sit thereat discreetly, arise temperately, please our friend duly, go to bed merrily, and sleep surely; for the joy of our Lord, Jesus Christ, Amen."

MEDIEVAL PRAYER

"There is a courtesy of the heart
It is akin to love
Out of it rises the
Purest in our outward behavior."

JOHANN WOLFGANG VON GOETHE

"laborare est orare—to work is to pray."

BENEDICTINE SAYING

"To live well is to love well, to show a good activity."

THOMAS AQUINAS

"Hands to Work and Hearts to God."

SHAKER MOTHER ANN LEE

PART 6

Love and Forgiveness

HOWEVER GOOD THE FRIENDSHIP, however intimate the relationship, every once in a while you will be hurt and have the opportunity to forgive, as you hope you will be forgiven when you give less than your best. Forgiveness allows us to escape from negative emotional entanglements with friends, lovers, and family. We can stop being the victim if we can be merciful. Compassionate forgiveness is not the denial of a negative act, it is the transcendence of it.

WHAT IS LOVING FORGIVENESS?

GOD'S LOVE IS GIVEN WITHOUT CONDITIONS. Nothing you can say or do—or that you have done in the past—can deny you His love. God's forgiveness is not the forgiveness that patronizes the one forgiven by saying (or implying) "You are bad, but I forgive you." His is the forgiveness that loves the whole of you, not just the bits approved of, or judged to be acceptable. His starting point is love, not condescension from a position of assumed superiority. You can be like God when you assume the same loving stance from which to forgive those who have acted against you. We forgive as Christians when we accept someone as he or she is and not as we would have them be. If who we would have them be is something different than they are, we neither love nor forgive. "I will love you if…or when…" is manipulative. Could you imagine Jesus saying this?

"Turn off the lights or keep them on.
Either way, I will see you,
Call me back or do not call me back.
Either way I will hear you.
Tell me yes or tell me no.
Either way, I will love you."

MARION WILLIAMSON

"When we love we want to forgive. It is so with God. Remember the tax gatherer (Luke 18) at the back of the Temple not daring to raise his eyes, in contrast to the Pharisee who prayed at the front, boasting of his accomplishments. it was not he who was justified, but the tax gatherer who prayed:

'Lord be merciful to me a sinner.'
that is a most marvellous prayer.
Who, praying that, can fail to
hear in his or her heart those
words of Our lord on the cross:
'Father, forgive them, they know
not what they do.' It is beautiful
to receive God's forgiveness, and it
is there for the taking."

CARDINAL BASIL HUME

FORGIVING YOURSELF

SOMETIMES IT IS NOT ENOUGH JUST TO BE forgiven by others; sometimes you have also to forgive yourself. To forgive and love yourself without forgetting the gravity of your actions. Being penitent and taking responsibility for past sins is a courageous and adult act of love that allows victims the right to be angry and empowers them to grant their own forgiveness, in time. In the gospels Christ's love was given to all who sincerely desired it. He welcomed sinners—and outcasts, the despised and diseased—in equal measure to the faithful and socially acceptable. It was the quality of their love or need that He responded to, not their social status, wealth, or how big a show of piety and ostentatious religious practice they adopted in an effort to impress him (read the parable of the Pharisee and the publican in Luke, chapter 18). No imitation of sincerity can fool Him since He is closer to you than the blood in your veins. He knows your secret self as well as your public self and loves you without reservation, so that you can have the confidence to love yourself.

"And Jesus knowing their thoughts said, Wherefore think ye evil in your hearts"

THE GOSPEL OF ST. MATTHEW 9:4

Casting the First Stone

"And early in the morning he came again into the temple, and all the people came unto him; and he sat down, and taught them.

And the scribes and the Pharisees brought unto him a woman taken in adultery; and when they had set her in his midst,

They say unto him, Master, this woman was taken in adultery, in the very act.

Now Moses in the law commanded us, that such should be stoned: but what sayest thou?

This they said, tempting him, that they might have to accuse him. But Jesus stooped down, and with his finger wrote on the ground, as though he heard them not.

So when they continued asking him, he lifted up himself and said unto them, He *that is without sin among you, let him first cast a stone at her.*

And again he stooped down, and wrote on the ground. And they which heard it, being convicted by their own conscience, went out one by one, beginning at the eldest, even unto the last: and Jesus was left alone, and the woman standing in the midst.

When Jesus had lifted up himself, and saw none but the woman, he said unto her, Woman where are those thine accusers? hath no man condemned thee?

She said, No man, Lord, And Jesus said unto her, Neither do I condemn thee: go, and sin no more."

THE GOSPEL OF ST. JOHN 8: 2–11

ANALYZING THE STORY

JESUS SHOWED BY EXAMPLE THAT WE SHOULD love the sinner and forgive the sin when he refused to join in the general condemnation of the woman brought to him to judge. Under Mosaic Law, an adulterous woman would be condemned to be stoned to death, so in bringing her before Jesus as he taught in the temple, the mob was testing His obedience to religious law. Jesus did not automatically condemn the woman according to law and tradition, but instead demanded that her accusers examine their own consciences by inviting whoever in the crowd had never committed a sin to go ahead and throw the first stone at the cowering woman. The angry mob was silenced as, of course, none could make such a claim. Each member of the crowd could recall instances in which they also had broken a law or two, even the priests. And so when Jesus looked up from his writing in the dust of the temple floor, he found all the accusers had wandered away. No one comes forth with the first stone because none are without sins and in need of God's forgiveness rather than condemnation. Jesus told the woman to go forth and sin no more, giving her a renewed chance to live a moral life by being forgiven and spared. The accusers were given a chance to reflect on their quick and hypocritical condemnation of another's failings when God knows all their own. This is not to say we should turn a blind eye to wrongdoing or sinful acts, but, as fellow sinners, that we forgive the sinner while abhorring the sin as we hope others will do for us.

BUT I'M NOT JESUS

FEW OF US MANAGE TO LOVE AND FORGIVE AS unconditionally as Jesus. For most of us, when certain boundaries are crossed, we are unable to love or forgive the transgressor. Regardless of the provocation, if you find yourself stuck with your pain and bitterness, ask God to bring about the forgiveness you cannot muster yourself. We all need God's grace and compassion to help us to see our judgmental agenda, and drop it. Love is being content with what is. You are not alone if you still have to work on that. Learning to forgive is a practice that can sometimes take a lifetime.

"Love is not patronizing and charity isn't about pity, it is about love. Charity and love are the same—with charity you give love, so don't just give money but reach out your hand instead."

MOTHER TERESA

BACK TO BASICS

CHRIST TELLS US WE SHOULD HAVE A SIMPLE heart if we want to reach God. "Except ye become... as little children, ye shall not enter into the kingdom of heaven." (Matthew 18:3). Children are born possessing an honest enthusiasm, innocence, and an openhearted attitude to love. They do not scheme or calculate ways to impress, nor manipulate to gain affection. With joyful faith and trust they hurl themselves into loving as their heart dictates. This is the quality Jesus recognizes and rewards time and time again in the gospels, when approached by those who whose faith has led them to be healed, or whom he has invited to forsake their past life and follow him. Accept and grant forgiveness for your sins and for those who have sinned against you and you are free to draw nearer to this perfect state of innocent love.

"And, behold, a woman, which was diseased with an issue of blood twelve years, came behind him, and touched the hem of his garment:
For she said within herself, If I may but touch his garment, I shall be whole. But Jesus turned him about, and when he saw her, he said, Daughter, be of good comfort; thy faith hath made thee whole. And the woman was made whole from that hour."

THE GOSPEL OF ST. MATTHEW 9: 20–22

I DON'T KNOW WHERE TO START

IT'S NEVER TOO LATE TO RETURN TO THE PATH
of love through forgiveness. Jesus teaches us
that God loves us unconditionally in the three
stories set out in the Gospel of St. Luke,
chapter 15. In these parables, or tales from
which we can take a moral, Jesus reminds us
that "there is joy in the presence of the
angels of God over one sinner that repents."
(Luke 15:10). First He tells the story of a
shepherd who has lost just one sheep from
his flock of one hundred. Though he still has
ninety-nine sheep who are safe, he searches
until the lost hundredth is found. When he

finds the lost sheep, the shepherd joyfully tells his friends and neighbors, and invites them to celebrate the good news. By this tale Jesus explained to his listeners, and through the gospels, to us, that it is never too late to come home to God, the shepherd, and that God will rejoice more over the person (or sheep) who had strayed than for all those who remained with Him. He also teaches that when good fortune comes our way it has not been given for us to savor alone. We should share good fortune with others, not hoard it away like a greedy miser. Next Jesus tells of a woman who, though she has ten valuable coins, turns her home upside down because a single one is lost. As with the shepherd, and his rediscovered sheep, she rejoices when the coin is found and invites her friends to share her joy.

The Prodigal Son

"And he said, A certain man had two sons: And the younger of them said to his father, Father, give me the portion of goods that falleth to me. And he divided unto them his living.

And not many days after the younger son gathered all together, and took his journey into a far country, and there wasted his substance with riotous living.

And when he had spent all, there arose a mighty famine in that land; and he began to be in want.

And he went and joined himself to a citizen of that country; and he sent him into his fields to feed swine.

And he would fain have filled his belly with the husks that the swine did eat: and no man gave unto him.

And when he came to himself, he said,

How many hired servants of my father's have bread enough and to spare, and I perish with hunger!

I will arise and go to my father, and will say unto him, Father, I have sinned against heaven, and before thee,

And I am no more worthy to be called thy son; make me as one of thy hired servants.

And he arose, and came to his father. But when he was yet a great way off, his father saw him, and had compassion, and ran, and fell on his neck, and kissed him.

And the son said unto him, father, I have sinned against heaven, and in thy sight, and am no more worthy to be called thy son.

But the father said to his servants, Bring forth the best robe, and put it on him; and put a ring on his hand, and shoes on his feet:

And bring hither the fatted calf, and kill it; and let us eat, and be merry:

For this my son was dead, and is alive again; he was lost, and is found. And they began to be merry.

Now his elder son was in the field: and as he came and drew nigh to the house, he heard musick and dancing.

And he called one of the servants, and asked what these things meant.

And he said unto him, Thy brother is come; and thy father hath killed the fatted calf, because he hath received him safe and sound.

And he was angry, and would not go in: therefore came his father out, and intreated him.

And he answering said to his father, Lo, these many years do I serve thee, neither transgressed I at any time thy commandment: and yet thou never gavest me a kid, that I might make merry with my friends:

But as soon as this thy son was come, which hath devoured thy living with harlots, thou hast killed for him the fatted calf.

And he said unto him, Son, thou art ever with me, and all that I have is thine.

It was meet that we should make merry, and be glad: for this thy brother was dead, and is a live again; and was lost, and is found."

THE GOSPEL OF ST. LUKE 15:11–32

ANALYZING THE STORY

THOUGH THIS THIRD STORY JESUS TELLS IS known as The Prodigal Son, it is as much the father's tale as the son's. The father's two sons have very different characters. The younger, a wastrel, pleads for his half of his inheritance now, before his father's death, to pay off debts amassed following a debauched lifestyle. The father heeds his younger son's plea and divides his fortune equally; half to the son who works hard and saves; half to the son who throws it all away on alcohol, women, and gambling. The young wastrel leaves home and lives a high life on his fortune until it runs out, while his hard-working, dutiful brother remains with his father, saving his share of the inheritance and continuing to work. Though his elder son works hard and loves him, the father patiently waits, hoping that one day his lost younger son will return home. Eventually the lost son, his inheritance exhausted, finds himself living in conditions worse than those his father's servants enjoy. Repenting of his foolishness and knowing he deserves no better treatment than a servant, he decides to go home and ask his father for mercy, and to hire him as a servant. The father rejoices and greets him tenderly and without recriminations. He tells his servants to prepare a feast to celebrate the return of his son with everyone. Again, the importance is stressed of a shared celebration at the return of a lost soul.

"Love is the power within us that affirms and values another human being as he or she is. Human love affirms that person who is actually there, rather than the ideal we would like him or her to be...."

ROBERT A. JOHNSON

PRAYERS, POEMS,

and

THOUGHTS

of

LOVE

"In your great love, O God, pardon our sins and restore a right spirit in our hearts. Guide us to love you with our whole being, so that our actions toward others might magnify you and that all may come to know grace upon grace as promised in your Word. Amen."

METHODIST PRAYER

"O Lord Jesus, because, being full of foolishness, we often sin and have to ask pardon, help us to forgive as we would be against us, nor dwelling on them in thought, nor being influenced by them in heart, but loving each other freely, as thou freely loved us; for thy name's sake. Amen."

CHRISTINA ROSSETTI

"To live of love, it is to know no fear;
No memory of past faults can I recall;
No imprint of my sins remaineth here;
The fire of Love divine effaces all.
O sacred flames! O furnace of delight!
I sing my safe sweet happiness to prove.
In these mild fires I dwell by day,
by night.
I live of love!"

ST. THERESE OF LISIEUX

"My Lord, I love You. My God, I am sorry. My God, I believe in You. My God, I trust You. Help us to love one another as You love us."

MOTHER TERESA

"Strange that so much suffering is caused because of the misunderstandings of God's true nature. God's heart is more gentle than the Virgin's first kiss upon the Christ. And God's forgiveness to all, to any thought or act, is more certain than our own being."

ST. CATHERINE OF SIENNA

LOVE IS GIVING EVERYTHING, WHILE HOLDING ON TO NOTHING

"Love does not ask for security, love just asks to be able to love. Nothing can stop our love. No matter if the person rejects us, or if they run away from us, they cannot stop us from loving them. Love asks for no guarantees. Love asks for no insurance. Love just wants to love, to give everything. In that love is a birthing, a fire that purifies. In that love is the greatness of being. In that love is all vision and purpose in life. The love that we give opens us to a new level of feeling, and a new level of joy."

CHUCK SPEZZANO

PART 7

Love Your Enemies

To BE ASKED TO LOVE AN ENEMY seems a pretty tall order, yet St. Matthew tells us we should love our enemies and pray for the people who annoy or wound us. He reminds us that it is easy to like those who like us, or those we are related to. The test of our love and Christian beliefs is to love those who, by their actions, make it clear they do not like us at all. These ideas may help you along the path.

LOVING EVERYONE

WOULD CHRIST HAVE SAID, I LOVE YOU AND YOU and you, but not you? Would God have lists of who is acceptable in His eyes and who is not? God is love. He does not use Love. He is love; and as Love, God is not partial, selfish, or conditional. God's love extends to our enemies as well as to us. Just as the rain falls on good and bad alike, God's love has no favorites. His love is beyond the dualistic concepts we are so caught up in: ideas such as like—don't like, good—bad, friend—enemy, brother—outsider. God's love encompasses all, saint and sinner. It just is. When armies claim to fight with God on their side, He is on both sides. He does not judge one cause better than another; nor does he call one faith more righteous than another; those are human conceits. God loves individuals whatever cause they espouse and whatever their badge of allegiance. God's love cannot be partial, though many cults and military generals throughout history have tried to appropriate it to justify their actions, or to persuade followers that their cause is more worthy than the other. Partisan love assigns limits to what would be acceptable and unacceptable. God does not take sides.

HOW DO I DO THAT?

ST. MATTHEW REMINDS CHRISTIANS TO STRIVE for perfection in imitation of God's perfection. God's universal love is an example to us all. Christ showed perfect love when he forgave those who wrongly accused, prosecuted, and tortured him. His love was so unconditional that he even asked God, his heavenly Father, to forgive those about to take his life. We must strive to love as God has taught us through His son Jesus Christ—unselfishly without preconditions or expectation of reward. Matthew tells his listeners they should love tax gatherers and Gentiles (socially despised groups of the time), while St. Luke says we should love all sinners, without specifying any groups in particular. Both disciples make the same point: Jesus taught that we should love without judgment and without counting the cost. It is easy to love those who love us, but if we would live in imitation of how He lived, we should make no distinction. Jesus welcomed all comers, whether Roman, tax gatherer, Pharisee, Gentile, prostitute, or any social outcast, good or evil. Love knows no division: its generosity embraces all.

> *"Love your enemies, do good unto*
> *them which hate you.*
> *Bless them that curse you, and pray*
> *for them which despitefully use you."*
> THE GOSPEL OF ST. LUKE 6: 27–28

"You have very little control over your feelings. That's why God didn't say, 'Like your enemy.' It's very difficult to like your enemy. But to love your enemies is different. Love is an act

of the will, where you can lovingly act even if you do not always feel loving. We tend to think love is a feeling, but it is not. Love is an action; love is something we do for others."

DESMOND TUTU WITH DOUGLAS ADAMS

UNDERSTANDING AN ENEMY

SOME PEOPLE HAVE SUFFERED SO MUCH THAT they have learned to shut down their feelings to be able to survive with some semblance of sanity. To reduce the pain, they have learned to split off feelings from events. Such individuals may subsequently find it hard to understand when their actions cause pain to others. As their own feeling nature has closed down, empathy or sympathy are no longer in their repertoire of emotions. Some children get no training in society's ground rules and no reward for considerate behavior, so we should not be surprised if they acquire different, more antisocial, life strategies to our own. To judge such people as you would judge yourself is inappropriate. We may prefer to believe such people are like us so we can hate them for their actions, but sympathy and love are more appropriate responses. Forgiving from a position of love does not condone a wrong act. Does any of this apply to you, too? Do you so fear dropping your own protective wall that you may never change. And does this mean you should never be forgiven? Consider the barriers you have to love and whether they are justified, but remember that God's love requires no preconditions and demands no prior apologies. It is given unconditionally.

"Yes, love (he thought again with perfect distinctness), but not that love that loves for something, to gain something, or because of something, but that love that I felt for the first time, when dying, I saw my enemy and yet loved him. I knew that feeling of love which is the very essence of the soul, for which no object is needed. And I know that blissful feeling now too. To love one's neighbors; to love one's enemies. To love everything—to love God in all His manifestations. Some one dear to one can be loved with human love; but an enemy can only be loved with divine love. And that was why I felt such joy when I felt that I loved that man. What

happened to him? Is he still alive?...
Loving with human love, one may pass
from love to hatred; but divine love can-
not change. Nothing, not even death,
nothing can shatter it. It is the very
nature of the soul....

Love is life. All, all that I understand,
I understand only because I love. All is,
all exists only because I love. All is bound
up in love alone. Love is God, and dying
means for me a particle of love, to go
back to the universal and eternal source
of love."

FROM "WAR AND PEACE", LEO TOLSTOY

LOVE AND RIGHTEOUS ANGER

WITH LOVE COMES CHOICE AND RESPONS-
ibility It is a mistake to believe that all anger
is bad, for example, when you are faced with
unkind acts. To be placid no matter the
provocation is unrealistic and certainly not
proof of a "good" person. Jesus threw the
moneylenders from the temple; he did not
ask them politely if they would mind leaving.
Righteous indignation is acceptable in the
appropriate circumstance. If you see cruelty
to a defenseless child, animal, or elderly
person, some righteous anger is entirely
appropriate. If you are in real and immediate

physical danger, you need to take action. How you express your need requires judgment and discretion. It helps no one if you place yourself at equal risk to the victim you intend to assist. You become the aggressor if your reaction is disproportionate to the threat. The spiritually developed person is one who knows and accepts all that they may be, including angry when the occasion demands it. Learn to use your anger with discrimination; enough, and no more.

"The sun, though it passes through dirty places, yet remains as pure as before."
FRANCIS BACON

PRAYERS, POEMS,

and

THOUGHTS

of

LOVE

"And one of the scribes came, and having heard them reasoning together, and perceiving that he had answered them well, asked him, Which is the first commandment of all?
And Jesus answered him, The first of all the commandments is, Hear, O Israel; The Lord our God is one Lord: And thou shall love the Lord thy God

with all thy heart, and with all thy soul,
and with all thy mind, and with all thy
strength: this is the first commandment.
And the second is like, namely this,
Thou shall love thy neighbor as thyself.
There is none other commandment
greater than these."

THE SERMON ON THE MOUNT, THE GOSPEL OF
ST. MARK 12: 28–31

"God did not deprive thee of the operation of his love, but thou didst deprive Him of thy co-operation. God would never have rejected thee, if thou hadst not rejected his love. O all-good God, thou dost not forsake unless forsaken, thou never takest away thy gifts until we take away our hearts."

ST FRANÇOIS DE SALES

"O Lord, the Author and Persuador of peace, love and goodwill, soften our hard and steely hearts, warm our frozen and icy hearts, that we may wish well to one another, and may be the true disciples of Jesus Christ. And give us grace even now to show forth that heavenly life, wherein there is no hatred, but peace and love on all hands, one toward another. Amen."

LUDOVICUS VIVES

PART 8

Love, Loss, and War

MOST OF THE TIME WE ARE engrossed in our our own private world—an interior life that permits little real contact with others. Love is close to us in all situations, but, surprisingly, when emotions are heightened by threat, love can seem closer. In times of adversity we are forced to be more aware of our fellow man, friend or foe. When the going gets rough, we are reminded of our shared fellowship and vulnerability and our need to help one another.

LOVE IN ADVERSITY

WE CAN ONLY MARVEL AT THE LOVE ORDINARY
people are capable of expressing in adversity. Survivors of wars and natural disasters
constantly attest to the selfless actions of
others—the kindnesses of strangers can
remain as vivid in the memory of survivors
as the recollections of horror. It seems
that whenever a tough situation prevails,
unremarkable men and women show extraordinary strength and faith in the Lord. Other
brave individuals have opposed oppressive
regimes and stood up to political dictators,
even under torture, imprisonment, or at the

cost of their lives, in order to achieve a better future for their countrymen. Such people are beacons of spiritual inspiration for all mankind. As Mother Teresa (a shining beacon herself) has stated, Christ's love is "always stronger than the evil in the world."

"We were born to make manifest the glory of God that is within us. It is not just in some of us; it is in everyone."

NELSON MANDELA

SEEING GOD IN OTHERS

OUR LIVES CAN BE CHANGED IN A MOMENT, for good or ill, by the actions of someone who remains unknown to us. Love—and God—is present in small acts and intimate moments whenever difficult circumstances force us to face our mortality. It may be a sympathetic hand on a shoulder, a sensitive smile, or the tear in the eye of a stranger that reminds us of the love that lies concealed beneath the veil of every face. Survivors of wars and other tragedies tell of individuals who have put their own life at risk, or even died, trying to help another; of the stranger whose acts of generosity and compassion made such a difference; of the dignity and courage of victims whose bravery in death deeply touched those who were spared. What a pity if we wait until we are in extremis before we become aware of the love that surrounds us. Every person longs to receive love and to give it, though for some, life dumped so much garbage on top it takes persistent giving to reach down to that core yearning. Never think it is too late to accept love and share your love with others.

"Works of love are always works of joy. We don't need to look for happiness: if we have love for others we'll be given it. It is the gift of God."

MOTHER TERESA

WHY DOES GOD
ALLOW SUFFERING?

IT HAS LONG BEEN A PUZZLE HOW A LOVING AND omnipotent God could permit suffering, or allow His people to take evil actions. The answer, I believe, is that He does not. We humans have been granted the freewill to act as we choose. God wants us to choose to love Him. But to be real, love cannot be coerced or manipulated, so we must have freedom of choice. Loving makes us better and stronger individuals. If we were incapable of choosing evil, it would be impossible to choose good. We would be like puppets. For meaningful choice to exist, we must allow the possibility of opposites. Thus, God is not the cause of evil or suffering, human beings are. God loves the sinner and the sinned against in equal measure. We find this hard to follow because we make conditional judgments all the time. God is beyond all dualities, while for humans, there is always an either/or. If an omnipotent or compassionate God could intervene to prevent the situation that has hurt us, it would be the action of a God who deprives mankind of freewill and takes sides. The choice to behave badly lies with us, not Him. Having freewill, we can choose to injure, steal from, or even kill one another, while our all-loving God looks on in a compassionate wonder at our refusal to choose love over hate.

"It never occurred to me to question God's doings or lack of doings while I was an inmate of Auschwitz, although of course I understand that others did… I was no less or no more religious because of what the Nazis did to us; and I believe my faith in God was not undermined in the least. It never occurred to me to associate the calamity we were experiencing with God, to blame Him, or to believe in Him less or cease believing in Him at all because he didn't come to our aid.

God doesn't owe us that, or anything. We owe our lives to Him. If someone believes God is responsible for the death of six million because he didn't somehow do something to save them, he's got his thinking reversed. We owe God our lives for the few or many years we live, and we have the duty to worship Him and do as He commands us. That's what we're here on earth for, to be in God's service, to do God's bidding."

AN AUSCHWITZ SURVIVOR

GOD SUFFERS, TOO

GOD MAY NOT INTERFERE WITH OUR CHOICES, but He suffers with us, since He is nearer to us than our own breath. His compassion for those who suffer is revealed in the support and comfort we receive following the negative effects of other people's choices. The urge to help a suffering person is God's love in action. Not in the sense that God manipulates the helper—He cannot do this either—but because we all bear the seeds of His love within us, and we are stirred to righteous action when we witness another person's pain.

"Bless them which persecute you: bless,
and curse not.
Rejoice with them that do rejoice, and
weep with them that weep.
Be of the same mind one toward another.
Mind not high things, but condescend to
men of low estate. Be not wise in your
own conceits.
Recompense to no man evil for evil.
Provide things honest in the sight of
all men.
If it be possible, as much as lieth in you,
live peaceably with all men."

ROMANS 12: 14–18

LOVE AND LOSS

WE ALL HAVE TO LEARN THE DIFFICULT LESSON of loss at some time in life. It may be the loss of a loved one to death, the pain of separation or divorce, the end of a valued friendship, or loss of things we value through breakage or theft. Letting go and accepting loss can be an opportunity to express love and gratitude for what was good, and offers us a chance to look forward to what the future has in store. Alternatively, it can be a time of bitterness and regret for disappointments and losses. The choice is ours. Some character types seem to blossom when faced with pain and adversity. Others are adept at sacrificing their own needs to the greater good. When we remember that everything we have stems from God, it becomes easier to accept what life serves up to us; the experiences we like and the ones we would rather avoid. We cannot control the experiences life presents, but we can exercise choice and control over how we deal with them.

COPING WITH
LOSS AND PAIN

THE LEAST PAINFUL AND MOST LOVING OPTION when you have to bear great loss or hurt, is to accept the things that cannot be changed and get on with those that can. It is futile to battle with what is. If your pain is the result of another person's action, know that only God can understand the processes that make another person act or behave as they do. The wrong that was done or said is over. No amount of bitterness or regret will change it, even a tiny bit. Vengeance would merely add to the wound you have suffered already and makes you no better than the cause of your pain, besides being in direct contradiction to Christ's teachings. We should turn the other cheek if someone casts a blow on one cheek, Jesus advises. If someone demands that we walk a mile as punishment, we must walk two. This is not masochism. It is to show our captor that God alone has dominion over us, not other men. We should be indifferent to the demands of men. We rise above attempts at persuasion by force through acceptance. Nothing is taken from us if we give it freely.

LEARNING ACCEPTANCE

THE LIFE OF JESUS IS OUR PRIME EXAMPLE of how to accept whatever occurs to us as God's will. Everything stems from God, including our ability to withstand this current test. We may not comprehend the reason for the events that now cause us pain; not yet, anyway. But with His grace we may do so in time. All that God requires from us right now is to decide where to go from here. The scenery or the players have moved unexpectedly, perhaps, but the play is still our own.

"God's love for us and our love for others is the single greatest motivating force in the world. And this love and the good it creates will always triumph over hatred and evil. But if you are to be true partners with God in the transfiguration of his world and help bring this triumph of love over hatred, of good over evil, you must begin by understanding that as much as God loves you, God equally loves your enemies."

DESMOND TUTU WITH DOUGLAS ADAMS

MAKING A CHOICE

YOU MUST DECIDE WHAT ACTIONS ARE ACCEPT-able or comfortable for you in coping with your loss or pain. As long as your choices do not violate anyone else's rights and choices, the options are entirely open. Trust yourself, and go with your own instinct. Take some quiet time to listen within to what you need and want to happen next, not what you believe others want from you—or what other people think you ought to want. When you allow yourself to be quiet and explore within, without any external pressures, you make yourself open to God's guidance. It's your job to live your life, not anyone else's. No one else has the same priorities or needs. However well meaning the advice or pressure others urge upon you, only you and God know what is right for you. Others have their own lives to unravel and truths to follow, and, who knows, in advising or pressurizing you, they may be doing just that. Accept that other people feel a need to advise you, and that love may prompt them to do so, but your need stems from God and your responses must be true to yourself and so to Him.

DEALING WITH DEATH

THE LOSS OF A LOVED ONE IS A PARTICULARLY painful trial. Following a death it is common to experience a number of heightened emotions. They occur in no particular order, but often include the feelings detailed opposite. If you are experiencing any of them, know that your trials are shared by all who grieve. Some people get stuck in one aspect of grieving—anger, denial, or a protective numbness perhaps—others veer back and forth between emotions more than once. It is perfectly reasonable to need spiritual guidance or professional counseling to restore your harmony.

What You Might Feel

❀ Disbelief or denial when faced with loss.

❀ Hope beyond realistic expectation that your loved one survived somehow.

❀ Anger at the deceased for having left you in this way.

❀ Anger at the agent that caused the loss.

❀ Anger at God for having taken this life.

❀ Grief and sorrow for yourself.

- Grief and sorrow for the person whose life was cut short.

- Numbness to all expression of feeling.

- Eventual acceptance that death happens in all families.

- Realization that death claims "good" and "bad" with dispassionate indifference (distinctions between good and bad being human in origin, not divine).

- Gradual incorporation of the loss into the revised life situation that has been thrust upon you.

- The ability to love again.

"Everything is God's to give and to take away, so share what you've been given, and that includes yourself."

MOTHER TERESA

ON DISASTERS

GOD DOES NOT DIRECT THE EARTH'S NATURAL forces to create disasters. He made the world and all its resources, but how the elements of His creation randomly interact thereafter is pure chance, or the result of human actions and choices. He made us intelligent enough to find the solutions to disputes and diseases, and to choose right actions over wrong ones. Whether we achieve our potential is up to us. We are mistaken if we believe God wills the acts that cause us sorrow. He feels with us when we grieve or suffer, and longs for us to turn to Him so he may show His love.

Remember, even—some might say especially—at times of great human tragedy and natural catastrophe, God is as close to us as the breath we take. We choose to forget Him or turn our face from Him, distracted by grief and shock, but he waits patiently, always ready to accept and support us as the father did his prodigal son. We might find him in the compassionate witness to the follies of mankind. He is also present in the positive community action that attends sad circumstances; in the neighbors, family, or strangers who offer help, support, and commiserations. God is not the author of willful or negligently painful events, though he witnesses all that mankind does with the freewill with which he has endowed us.

FEELING ANGRY WITH GOD

LOSS TO DEATH OR REJECTION CAN AFFECT OUR attitudes to God and faith. Our thoughts may be despairing, *"How can a loving God allow this?"* or angry, *"How could He take this innocent when so many worthless individuals remain alive?"* We may blame God for deserting us in our hour of need, *"Why has this happened to me?"* It is OK to be angry with Him. He understands our motivation and will not retaliate. Bitter regret following a negative experience is understandable; we have all known suffering. But God is not to blame. We need to change our understanding of God.

He is not the motivator of a wicked or sinful act. He gave us freewill to act as we choose. He also gave us our sense of outrage and injustice.

"Here is my secret. I tell it to you with an openness of heart that I doubt I shall ever achieve again. I pray that you are in a quiet room as you hear these words. My secret is that I need God—that I am sick and can no longer make it alone. I need God to help me give, because I no longer seem to be capable of giving; to help me to be kind, as I no longer seem capable of kindness, to help me love, as I seem beyond being able to love."

DOUGLAS COUPLAND

WHEN TO BLAME

IF BLAME IS DESERVED AFTER A TRAUMATIC event, it belongs with the humans involved and the choices they made, rather than with God. Our suffering arises from random and disinterested bad luck. To blame God is to make Him into a vindictive God rather than a compassionate and loving Father. You probably were not singled out for this negative experience. It isn't personal. Life is not fair or unfair. It just is. People get hurt or robbed or killed and someone will always feel it happened to the wrong person. Angry, bitter blame is really denial and rage at the random sequence of events that lie between your happiness and misery. Might not blame be inappropriate? When can we say someone actually makes a choice to do ill? In the moment of a hurtful act, or as a mindless, spontaneous product of a lifetime's conditioning and opportunities? If a few rare individuals do express evil intent without remorse, they make that choice from their own freewill, and we should not blame God. He grieves at their decision as well as at the pain they inflict on others. If there are no redeeming explanations for a person's negative actions, to add the burden of your urge for retribution or revenge to the situation helps no one. It does not impinge on the instigator in any way; he or she is already beyond reach. But carrying out an act of revenge does damage you, adding to the pain caused you in the first place.

COPING WITH ANGER
AND BITTERNESS

IF WE CAN'T APPORTION BLAME, THEN WHAT CAN we do with feelings of anger or bitterness? Though it might be tempting, do not act out your rage upon others; that just passes the misery further down the chain from where it started, maybe generations before. Simply accept that you feel as you do. Do not deny it or feel guilty for it. Feelings just arrive, unbidden, like the sunshine or rain. And, like the weather, their cause is equally impersonal and will pass in time. Do not listen to those who advise you not to weep when weeping is what you need, or who tell you not to rage, if anger is within you. What they are really saying is that your strength of feeling makes them uncomfortable. You have enough to deal with right now without taking on the responsibility of how others are reacting to your grief or sorrow. You feel as you do. That is your right and your truth. Seek the company of those who can support you through this difficult period of adjustment. Try not to scare off the people who want to help. They mean well, even if their methods may be clumsy. God longs to embrace you and comfort you through the help you can find in others. It might help to explore some of the issues raised by the thoughts set out on pages 276–77.

Thoughts to Ponder

❧ Your feelings of anger and hurt may be entirely appropriate, but to direct them at God is to deny the real agency: our human freewill.

❧ Blaming God for bad things also denies the world we have been given, in which everything changes, decays, and dies away. Humans are not separate from that natural process.

❀ To demand God's intervention implies we are helpless puppets on whom God acts as the puppeteer. If He intervenes to prevent or protect, we become no more than His playthings.

❀ God allows us to make our own mistakes and triumphs.

❀ The world contains great beauty and goodness, even though its people are not always perfect.

ACCEPTING SADNESS

THE SAD REALITY IS THAT OUR LOVED ONES may just have been in the wrong place at the wrong time. No act, or failure to act, on our part could in any way have contributed to or prevented that random bad luck. It happened. That is the reality of it. To berate ourselves, or others, from a need to apportion blame or to assume guilt, is just nonsensical. The child who has lost a beloved parent should not be made to believe God needed that parent more than the child does, for instance—being told that makes a child feel guilty for not wanting her parent enough. A compassionate God is not responsible for depriving you of a loved one, of instigating natural disasters to make you suffer, or inciting hatred in the heart of a terrorist that leads to violence. You may feel deserving of better luck, but God does not distribute luck. We make our own. The Bible tells us God notices when a single sparrow falls to the ground, so how could He be unaware when a human being falls! But awareness is not the same as causation. Awareness equates with compassionate sympathy, not with benign or malevolent manipulation.

OFFERING LOVING SUPPORT

IF YOU WANT TO OFFER LOVING SUPPORT TO someone who is bereaved or emotionally wounded in some other way, the most helpful thing you can do is bear witness to the pain. Keep your experiences to yourself, however comparable they may seem. This moment is about being a loving witness to the person before you who is experiencing pain. Recall times when others tried to comfort you by relating their own histories; did it help? To listen without judging and without dragging in your own history is a compassionate skill. Too often listeners don't want to hear talk that seems to upset the speaker, so they either avoid or change the subject, or try to cheer up the sad person. This denies the natural grieving process. What we really say when we do this is, *"I don't know how to deal with your pain so please stop making me feel uncomfortable."* The grieving person needs to share his or her tumble of thoughts and memories, and, yes, sometimes doing so makes them sad, but in allowing someone to reflect on memories or replay a tragedy, you honor a need; the painful tumult will eventually subside. Perhaps after an appropriate period of adjustment, this grief may even inspire an intensified trust and faith in God.

What to Do

❁ The most you can do is be available to listen and keep open a loving space to encompass the pain and grieving person.

❁ If someone needs to rail against God, He can take it; you need not defend Him.

❁ Does the wounded person repeatedly asks unanswerable questions of you? You are not expected to know the answers, simply to be God's ears in this moment of anguish.

- If you don't know what to say, a touch of the hand in sympathy, a handkerchief for the tears, and an enquiry into how the person is getting on is enough.

- The gift of a meal or help with chores, the silent gift of time and attention; these are the loving acts of a Christian.

"The fruit of silence is
PRAYER
The fruit of prayer is
FAITH
The fruit of faith is
LOVE
The fruit of love is
SERVICE"

MOTHER TERESA

ACTING GROWN-UP

IT IS THE MARK OF AN ADULT WHEN LOSSES, disappointments, and setbacks can be met with love, even though we are hurting. We are not responsible for any one else's life—that is purely a matter for God and that individual— but we are responsible for how we conduct ourselves; for the effect our words and deeds have upon others. If unpalatable decisions really must be made, we have a responsibility as Christians to exercise compassion in their implementation, to deal with others as we would want to be dealt with ourselves if the places were reversed.

PRAYERS, POEMS,

and

THOUGHTS

of

LOVE

*"You are love
and you see all the suffering,
injustice, and misery,
which reign in this world.
Have pity, we implore you,
on the work of your hands.
Look mercifully on the poor,
the oppressed, and all who are heavy laden
with error, labor and sorrow.
Fill our hearts with deep compassion for those
who suffer
and hasten the coming of your kingdom
of justice
and truth."*

EUGÈNE BERSIER

"Love bade me welcome; yet my soul
drew back,
Guilty of dust and sin.
But quicky-eyed Love, observing me grow
slack
From my first entrance in,
Drew nearer to me, sweetly questioning
If I lack'd anything.

'A guest', I answered, 'worthy to be here.'
Love said, 'You shall be he.'
'I, the unkind, ungrateful? Ah, my dear,
I cannot look on Thee.'
Love took my hand and smiling did reply,
'Who made the eyes but I?'"

GEORGE HERBERT

"Be happy in the moment, that's enough. Each moment is all we need, not more. Be happy now and if you show through your actions that you love others, including those who are poorer than you, you'll give them happiness too. It doesn't take much—it can be just giving a smile. The world would be a much better place if everyone smiled more. So smile, be cheerful, be joyous that God loves you."

MOTHER TERESA

"Love seeketh not itself to please,
nor for itself hath any care,
but for another gives its ease,
and builds a Heaven in Hell's despair."

WILLIAM BLAKE

"I asked for Peace—
My sins arose,
And bound me close,
I could not find release.

I asked for Truth—
My doubts came in,
And with their din
They wearied all my youth.

I asked for Love—
My lovers failed,
And griefs assailed
Around, beneath, above.

I asked for Thee—
And Thou didst come
To take me home
Within Thy heart to be."

D. M. DOLBEN

"Love is indestructible,
Its holy flame forever burneth;
From heaven it came,
to heaven returneth."

ROBERT SOUTHEY

"I will love thee, O Lord, my strength...
For thou wilt light my candle: the Lore
my God will enlighten my darkness."

FROM PSALM XVIII

"Not with doubting, but with assured consciousness do I love thee, O Lord. Thou didst strike my heart with thy word and I loved thee. And the heavens too, and the earth and all therein, manifestly on every side they bid me love thee; nor cease to say so unto all, that there may be no excuse....

But what do I love when I love Thee? Not grace of bodies, nor the beauty of the seasons, nor the brightness of the light, so gladsome to these eyes; nor inexhaustible melodies of sweet song, nor the fragrant smell of flowers, of ointments and spices, not manna and honey, not limbs accept

able to embracements of the flesh. None
of these love I when I love my God: and
yet I love a kind of light, and of melody
and of fragrance, a kind of food, and a
manner of embracement, when I love my
God; the embracement, food, fragrance,
melody, and light of my inner man:
where there shineth unto my soul what
space containeth not, and there soundeth
what time snatcheth not, and there
smelleth what breath disperseth not, and
there tasteth what eating cloyeth not, and
there clingeth what satiety divorceth not.
This is it which I love when I love
my God."

*"Our way is where God knows
And Love knows where:
We are in Love's hand to-day."*

ALGERNON CHARLES SWINBURNE

*"By love may He be gotten and holden,
by thought never."*

JULIAN OF NORWICH

"Thou hast made me for thyself
O Lord and my heart will never rest
until it rests in thee."

ST. AUGUSTINE

"To God the Father, who first loved us,
and made us accepted in the Beloved;
To God the Son who loved us,
and washed us from our sins
in his own blood;
To God the Holy Ghost,
who sheds the love of God abroad
in our hearts
be all love and all glory for time and for
eternity. Amen"

BLESSING BY THOMAS KEN

BIBLIOGRAPHY

All Bible quotes are taken from the King James Version.

At the Heart of the World by Cormac Murphy-O'Connor, Cardinal Archbishop of Westminster, Darton, Longman and Todd Ltd., 2004.

Enchanted Love—The Mystical Power of Intimate Relationships by Marion Williamson, Rider, 1999.

God Has a Dream: a vision of hope for our time by Desmond Tutu with Douglas Abrams, Doubleday, 2004.

God Outside the Box: why spiritual people object to christianity by Richard Harries, SPCK, 2002.

Handbook for the Soul edited by Richard Carlson and Benjamin Shield, Judy Piatkus Publishers Ltd., 1995.

If it Hurts it Isn't Love; Secrets of Successful Relationships by Chuck Spezzano, Hodder and Stoughton, 1999.

Life After God by Douglas Coupland, Simon & Schuster, 1994.

Meditations and Devotions by Cardinal Newman (John Henry Newman), Longman, 1907.

Traditional Hymns, Ebury Press, 1996.

The Book of Peace: finding the spirit in a busy world by Mother Teresa, excerpted from *A Simple Path* compiled by Lucinda Vardey, Rider 1996.

The Inner Life: Book Two—On Inner Consolation by Thomas à Kempis, Penguin Books Great Ideas Series, 2004.

The Mystery of Love by Cardinal Basil Hume O.S.B., Darton, Longman and Todd Ltd., 2004.

The Psychology of Romantic Love by Robert A. Johnson, Arkana Paperbacks, 1984.

When Bad Things Happen to Good People by Harold S. Kushner, Schocken Books, 1981.

Yes, there is Somthing You Can Do. 150 Prayers, Poems, and Meditations for Times of Need by Jamie C. Miller, Fair Winds Press, 2003.